The Pagan Thing: aspects of Modern Paganism.

Pete Jennings © 2021

GRUFF BOOKS

PETE JENNINGS
12 CARLTON CLOSE, GREAT YELDHAM,
HALSTEAD, ESSEX CO9 4QJ
TEL 01787 238257 / 07778 366469
www.gippeswic.org
gippeswic@btinternet.com

This book is dedicated to Druid Emma Restall Orr, who makes me think, and has won my respect.

To Sarah
Happy Paths
Pete

Index

"Learn from yesterday, live for today, hope for tomorrow. The important thing is not to stop questioning."

Albert Einstein

Chapter 1. Thinking about different ideas.

Are you an established Pagan or thinking about becoming one? Are you drawn to a spiritual path for thinking people? It does not suit those with closed minds or wanting it already worked out by somebody else. Pagans have to decide what is right for themselves, or others will fill their open minds with rubbish. It may not be the same for any other Pagan, but that doesn't matter, you have the freedom to choose. As a spiritual path that prides itself on being open-minded, we should take a regular audit of our opinions which should be subject to change based on new information, personal experience or meditation. Otherwise, we shall become part of a personal orthodoxy, an anathema to most Pagans.

Defining the un-definable

This book isn't really how to do things. There are already more than enough of those available that you can shake a wand at. Nor is it an attempt to tell you what Paganism is or to define whether you are a Pagan or not. Instead, this book helps you think about some critical Pagan topics and applies to whichever path you are interested in, be it Druid[1], Witch, Heathen, Shaman, Eclectic or whatever one of many ways of being ignites your passion. I hope that it will also be helpful to academic researchers seeking fresh and alternative texts to those previously available to them.

Although few Pagans identify themselves as such, most of those groupings are classed by others as 'pantheists', which means that the gods and goddesses are part of nature, so the deity is immanent in nature. (Adler 2006, p.23) 'Immanent' implies that the gods are all over the universe and help to sustain it. The reverse of this would be 'transcendent in which the god is the creator of the universe and placed above it. 'Animism' is yet another descriptive term applied to Pagans and denotes a reverence and belief that everything has a spirit form, from trees, rocks and pools to animals and humans. Some Pagans hold that belief, but not all.

Trying to define Paganism has defeated and frustrated more refined minds than mine. The movement is anarchistic and adverse to labelling, authoritative texts or leaders. The problem is that most terminology and theology is centred upon the idea of a single monotheistic god, whereas Pagans acknowledge at least a god plus goddess. Many have pantheons of many gods and goddesses, sometimes seen as independent entities in their own right. This is known as 'polytheistic' or 'worshipping many gods.' Others see all gods as aspects of one god, all goddesses as aspects of one goddess. Some of the witchcraft groups that grew out of radical feminism (particularly in the USA) regard the Goddess as the pair's ascendant. Such covens are usually labelled as 'Dianic.' This seems to have been a less popular idea elsewhere, where god & goddess are regarded upon equal terms.

If all this seems a lot of irrelevant waffle, that is fine! It would help if you defined yourself and not be overly influenced by other's theories.

The Pagan Thinker

Make up your own mind.

I do not have the right to tell anyone what to do, how to act, or think. However, I believe it may help give some essential topics for modern Pagans to think about. After all, most Pagans from my experience would ignore my instructions and reach their own conclusions. When I mention my own opinions, I accept that although they are alright by me, they are rarely in line with what many other Pagans think and may not be appropriate for anyone else. With experience and further information, I reserve the right to change my opinions in future. I have included many quotations to show other people's opinions, but I do not necessarily think that they are any more correct than mine. They are there to stimulate your mind. For researchers' benefit, my printed opinions do not represent all Pagan thoughts any more than the Pope represents all Christian thoughts.

I speak from the experience of becoming interested in Pagan ideas in the late 1960s and continued to read about them. I did not start undertaking any active involvement until the late 1980s. Since then, I have been a Pagan activist in the U.K., organising groups, moots, conferences, lecturing and writing, and mixing with a broad cross-section of modern Pagans. I served as Media Officer and later President of The Pagan Federation. It is the largest general umbrella organisation for Pagans across the U.K. and Europe. My particular path as a Heathen draws upon Anglo Saxon & Viking sources. I count Heathen as a specific type of Pagan, but many other Heathens may disagree, categorising themselves differently. I have many friends (and probably a few enemies!) across the whole spectrum of paths generally known as Paganism.

It has been a frequent observation that generally, Pagans are more likely to problem solve by ritual methods than to overthink and plan. That is a gross misrepresentation of many modern Western Pagans, but it has an element of truth. While some take themselves away from everyday life to meditate on the big picture or even set out to wild places to isolate themselves from the mundane world, they do not seem to be in the majority. That seems unfortunate: if you are not thinking about the basis of your personal Pagan path, who will? The danger is that someone else will do it for you. Isn't that one of the things that Pagans rebel against? Having someone else serve up pre-prepared beliefs on a platter is the first step towards having a hierarchy and literature that restricts your views to a one size fits all, homogenised mix, devoid of passion or individuality.

When I use the term 'modern Pagans', I am referring to Pagans living now in 2021 and can interchangeably use the term 'contemporary Pagans.' I am not referring to 'modernism' and 'post modernism'. However, the advent of the current movement originated at the start of the 'postmodernist' era in the mid-1960s, when many old ideas and social norms were being challenged, including religion, social status, music, fashion, sexuality and politics.

There are some Pagans who are content to go along with the general flow whilst not thinking about what drives and contributes to that flow. They may live their lives quietly or turn up to Pagan events and enjoy them without ever wanting more out of life than that. Like many, they may not see the need to follow any specific path and remain eclectic in their choice of beliefs. Good luck to them! I wish I could live a simpler life and not have to figure out my life's motivations and basis. It would be a lot less stressful to be just enjoying the experience of living in the moment. Still, self-reflection is an ongoing, habitual process that I started as a counsellor and social worker in my working life many years ago. Having been retired for a couple of years now, I guess I have more time to contemplate what is going on and offer my thoughts to others, not as advice but as a stimulus to their personal growth. Goddess forbid that you take me as a good example: I'm more a dreadful warning! By disagreeing with me, you may find it easier to discover what you think is correct.

The Pagan Thinker

A critical issue to remember within such soul searching is that we as humans are not perfect. Neither are we the same person each day. We do not behave as well when we are frightened, ill, stressed or angry. Our sense of cool logic may disappear into more visceral 'fight or flight' behaviours. Try not to beat yourself up about that: you can have the most well thought out aims, morals, non-confrontational behaviour and divine inspiration, but there are always triggers that will result in you falling short of your lofty ideals. Regrettably, I frequently fail to live up to the standards I try to set myself. I start the day with good intentions, but it often goes downhill when I get out of bed. At least if your objectives are well thought out beforehand, you will have something to aim for, and the process of trying to achieve them will be positive in itself, even if you do not totally succeed. This journey is also part of the process of 'higher magic' that I shall address later in this work.

To offer some clarity, I have divided the topics that I believe are important to consider into separate chapters. Inevitably though, all of them are interrelated and overlap. The alternative was to offer some impenetrable unstructured stream of consciousness, so be thankful for small mercies. The way we relate to our deities, the world, and our communities depend upon our personal theology. The frequent disregard for fundamental theology within Paganism (as opposed to academia) is an unfortunate deficit. Maybe we try too hard at 'doing Paganism' rather than first thinking about how and why we should do it in the first place. This book is an attempt to set up some initial, faltering steps into that process.

Chapter 2. Thinking about Gods & Goddesses?

The nature of religions

Scientists such as Bruce Hood[2], a professor at Bristol University, and Foster (2010) tell us that humans are 'hot wired' to need a belief system. Few of us are born Pagan these days, although a few second and third-generation offspring of the pioneers from the 1950s onwards are appearing. So why choose a spiritual path that is hard to find, difficult to follow and at odds with much of modern society, especially when there are so many other easier choices out there? I suppose it comes down to what people want out of any religion?

Most religions give a set of instructions to live by along the lines of "be nice to each other and play nicely, children." Faith may give a sense of belonging, a feeling of being thankful for what you have, and a promised life after death. It may even provide some form of 'supernatural help' for those who get it right and punish the bad guys that you are powerless to stop. What most religions do not give you (even if they claim otherwise) is free will. It will be ruled by some sort of leadership and prescribed by some kind of books. I guess those last two features are where Paganism scores: make up your own mind and do not have any authoritative texts!

Why have any form of religious or spiritual life at all? You can be an excellent person, caring, giving, fair-minded, generous etc., without any respect for gods, e.g. Humanist, Agnostic or Atheist. You can also be the nastiest bit of work in creation and insist that you follow a particular religion or even use that to justify your actions.

> "As scientific understanding has grown, so our world has become dehumanised. Man feels himself isolated in the cosmos, because he is no longer involved in nature and has lost his emotional "unconscious identity" with natural phenomena. These have slowly lost their symbolic implications. Thunder is no longer the voice of an angry god, nor is lightning his avenging missile. No river contains a spirit, no tree is the life principle of a man, no snake the embodiment of wisdom, no mountain cave the home of a great demon. No voices now speak to man from stones, plants, and animals, nor does he speak to them believing they can hear. His contact with nature has gone, and with it has gone the profound emotional energy that this symbolic connection supplied."
>
> (C.G. Jung, 1968)

The above text was written in 1968 by an important figure in psychology but seems just as relevant today. Following Freud's work, Jung was the first psychologist to declare that the human psyche is "by nature religious" and gave us essential knowledge on archetypes.

Why become a Pagan?

Many Pagans are initially drawn to the spiritual paths because of an interest in the environment.

> *Giddens (1991) attributes the reason for identifying with Paganism to environmentalism. The idea of having an interest in nature as a definition of Paganism is a key factor when attempting to understand what it means to be Pagan. The official U.K. definition of Paganism has been outlined by the Pagan Federation (2017) as: "a polytheistic or pantheistic nature-worshipping religion", which therefore includes any religion whose key belief is in the   inherent love for nature, or 'mother Earth' (Moreton, 2009; Gallagher, 2013). Due to the diversity present in Paganism, it is referred to as an 'umbrella' faith (Crowley, 2014) that includes (but is not limited to): Wicca, Witchcraft, Druidry (Adler, 1987), Asatru, Heathenry, Norse and Hedgewitch.*
>
> (Law, D. 2017 p.4-5)

However, that is an over-simplification of the process: one can, after all, have a strong interest or take practical steps towards care of the environment without any religious path. Some may become interested in Paganism through other routes.

The Feminine Divine

Many women (especially, but not exclusively in the USA) were initially attracted to witchcraft via the Radical Women's Rights movement of the 1960s and 1970s. They sought empowerment in a non-patriarchal religion.

"Pagan theologians like Starhawk indeed define the 'ancient' religion or witchcraft as 'goddess religion'. The goddess in thus not only pantheistically equated with the world or with 'reality' but is seen also as immanent in both humans and the natural world. The world, Starhawk writes, 'is the manifestation of the goddess', and this 'model' of the goddess, who is immanent in nature, 'fosters respect for the sacredness of all living things'"

(Morris, B. 2006 p275)

Some all-female 'Dianic' covens were born to worship and possibly create or recreate a matriarchal form of witchcraft. The Goddess Worship culture has spread out from the USA into the rest of the Western world, with its local variants. E.g. 'The Fellowship of Isis' and the 'Elen of the Ways' organisations. (Wise, C. 2015) In the various surveys and census across Europe and the USA, more women register as Pagans and Witches than men. There was a belief in an ancient matriarchal society ruled by women based upon archaeological finds such as the Venus of Willendorf. Academic thinking has veered away from this idea now, if not refuted it entirely. The existence of female goddess figures does not necessarily imply that women ruled or had equal status.

Some of the ideas of gender in religion have been investigated and acted upon in more recent times by the LGBT+ community, who find a general Pagan acceptance of diverse sexuality and gender identity to be a refreshing change from the disapproval of other mainstream religions. However, such issues seem to be having a less welcome reception elsewhere. For example, they have caused divisions within the Church of England over attitudes to openly gay priests, having just got over the hurdle of partly accepting the introduction of heterosexual female clergy. That is not directly our concern as

Pagans, but it does underline the differences we may have in engaging with some other religions in Interfaith discussions.

British Witchcraft travelled to the USA and elsewhere, and the Radical Feminist movement appreciated its placement of a positive and leading role for women. Some influential American female writers interpreted that in their own way and re-exported it to England, sometimes through the network of women they joined at the 1960s Greenham Common Peace Camp or the 'Re-claiming Tradition' of the influential Starhawk and Diane Baker, incorporating ideas of Z. Budapest and the Feri Tradition of the Andersons. This Greenham camp was a protest against a nuclear missile-equipped military base, but was unusual in that men were not welcomed as part of the process in general. (Some men were allowed to provide external childcare and other support services.) The model of Pagan mythology that was frequently adopted was the Greek Elysian Mysteries, with the goddess Persephone to the fore. But, as Mueller demonstrates, what they tended to miss out on was that Hades raped her to take her to the underworld. This fact seems to have been sanitised in many versions, probably because it is contrary to the Goddess being seen as controlling her destiny.

> *"There is irony in feminist Neo-pagans' habit to "look the other way as the god rapes the goddess," given the initial factors that led many women in the 1970s and continue to lead women to leave their families' religious traditions for the Goddess spirituality movement."*

(Mueller, M. 2005 p46)

The Male Divine

Whilst I acknowledge the mistakes and misogyny of thousands of years of patriarchy, I also believe that it is an over-reaction and error to replace it with a matriarchy that in many cases excludes half the population, such as myself, i.e.

men. Some men have told me that they find their role in some forms of Witchcraft (but not other Pagan paths) as 'confused' or 'insubstantial.' They are needed to represent the Goddess consort, but otherwise feel 'second class citizens' of the movement. Some British men did form all-male groups, following the 'Iron John' book by John Bly (1990) or 'Merlin Mysteries' (2009) promoted by RJ Stewart. However, these never seemed to gather much impetus and were generally short-lived in the UK. Scarlet Jory (2016) examined male stereotypes moving between Christian and Pagan men's groups in America.

> *"In an ethnography looking at gender and Wicca, socio-cultural gender roles are learned and become baggage in the religious lives of Pagans trying to define roles they no longer easily identify with."*

(Jory, 2016 p11)

Identity
Some individuals eschew Paganism because they feel it can shock and annoy their family and will give them some air of 'cool.' The very word 'Witch' still has the power to raise fear amongst many otherwise seemingly sensible people, as they focus on the broomstick flying, wart encrusted Halloween cackling hag imagery. (Apologies to any of my friends who fit that description!) Hutton (2017) constructed a whole book around the idea of a history of fear, from ancient times to the present. The individuals drawn in for a touch of infamy tend to fall away reasonably quickly if ridiculed or laughed at. Some may be drawn into transient fashions of whatever is the 'flavour of the month' when they become involved, from Enochian magic to techno-shamanism. Still, some will stubbornly persist and may later even embrace a path for more enlightened reasons.

Writing about Pagan identity for the *British Library Newsletter*, Prof.Denise Cush is Emeritus Professor of Religion and

Education, Bath Spa University. She raised several valid points:

> *"Identifying as Pagan is becoming more acceptable than it was in the middle of the previous century, and there are Pagan schoolteachers and members of the police force. The Pagan Federation joined the Religious Education Council in 2011 and the Inter-Faith Network in 2015. However, there is still something of a 'countercultural' feel about Pagan identity, stemming in part from its association with witchcraft (illegal until 1951), the 'hippies' of the   1960s and various anti-war and environmental protests. Women find the stress on Goddess(es) and the roles of witch or priestess empowering compared to the patriarchal attitudes of many older religions, and those who identify as lesbian, gay, bisexual or transgender generally feel welcome among Pagans. Young people identifying as witches or Pagans interviewed by the author found in Pagan identity a source of self-esteem and a vocabulary with which to interpret their experience. They also found that Pagan rituals gave them a sense of control and thus reduced anxiety. Many Pagans talk about 'coming home', finding a name and a community that shares the views and feelings they already had. As a relatively new tradition, many first identified as Pagans as teenagers or adults, but as children are increasingly born into Pagan families, it will be interesting to see how the Pagan community (or rather communities plural) develops in the future."*

(Cush, D. 2019)

Whether the reasons for being drawn to Paganism outlined by Prof. Cush resound with you is a matter to consider. Others may find themselves drawn to Paganism through other interests, such as love of nature, environmental issues, feminism, an interest in history or even reaction against beliefs previously held or taught. It may even be listening to particular bands, watching horror films or reading those dreadful Dennis Wheatley occult thrillers. Warning Wheatley fans: you will not find many virgin sacrifices on the actual altars, and attaining mystic power over others is more complicated than it sounds!

Neither will you get your religion served up conveniently on a plate. Author of the seminal American Pagan book *'Drawing Down the Moon'* (1979), the late Margot Adler said:

> *"I'm not sure that it's [Paganism] ever going to become a major religion. That's because you have to have a certain kind of strength and sense of self to be a Pagan. Paganism does not give you 'The Answer.' It doesn't claim there is one truth, or that you're gonna get it all solved by just believing this or that. That means that you have to be comfortable with living with confusion, multiplicity, and the idea that there are many truths and many answers. That's not so easy for a lot of people. They want answers."*

(Adler, M. 2001 p. 29)

There is an ironic development in the Mormon Church of Latter Day Saints. A new subculture has recently formed by members of both genders embracing forms of witchcraft and other esoteric beliefs. They feel these are in tune with some of the folk magic elements of their Church's creation (including a Mother Goddess) and can integrate them into their religious worldview whilst remaining Mormon. (Morehead, J., 2006)

Entry

A common way of entry into Paganism has been related to me so often as to almost become a cliché. With slight variations, it follows this form: *"I had a load of ideas and found out that they were what is called Paganism. I didn't know until then that I was a Pagan, but now that I have found others thinking roughly the same things, it is like coming home."* Over the years, I have heard this explanation repeatedly, although I have also heard of other processes for people becoming Pagans. As a movement against proselytising to others, it may explain the rapid growth despite no 'outreach' work. However, the Polish academics Adam Anczyk & Matouš Vencálek have provided a balanced and detailed investigation of this phenomenon and shown that it is also a part of some other religious conversion processes:

> *"The so-called "homecoming" is one of the most (if not the most) popular ways of depicting the process of becoming a follower of Neo-Paganism found in literature, from Margot Adler's classical Drawing Down the Moon (1979) to contemporary authors, like Graham Harvey. It is interesting that "homecoming" simultaneously occurs in Neo-Pagan literature, as the common way of becoming Pagan, seen as opposite to the process of conversion (usually as a rapid change of religious beliefs). The critique of the "homecoming" defined in the academic field concentrates on showing that there is a possibility it may be more a theological notion, rather than a model of religious change to contemporary Paganism."*

> (Anczyk, A. & Vencálek, M. 2013 p.161)

They also show the difference (and abhorrence) of many Pagans to the label of 'New Age', the valuable differences across Baltic states and cite the important English academic, Graham Harvey. I think it is worth reflecting on his exact words:

> *"Pagans do not speak about realizing the correctness of Pagan beliefs, or of experiences which require rapid changes of world-view. More typically they discover that the name for their existing sort of spirituality is Paganism. They find that they are not alone in the world but that there are books, groups and*

worldwide web sites devoted to the exploration of this spirituality."

(Harvey, G., 1999, p.234).

The relief of the 'newbie' is often due to finding it challenging to fit in anywhere before, especially in their formative years at school. Doreen Valiente (1961), the woman who Prof. Hutton called *"the greatest single female figure in the modern British of witchcraft"* (Heselton, 2016 p.xv), certainly found it hard there:

"Witches are those who do not conform. In school, they are not the child who can answer all the questions; they are the child who asks all the questions, especially the ones teacher can't answer."

(Valiente cited by Heselton, 2016 p.33-34)

It is what happens next to these 'new Pagans' that concerns us here. Some will accept what they have learnt and carry on with their lives. Others will become the epitome of the 'enthusiastic new convert' and want to attend events, join a coven, buy books, chat excitedly for hours and purchase all the equipment they think they will need.

Already, they are in that 'doing' phase, and there is no equivalent to the Christian Alpha course to offer them guidance. It can sometimes be down to chance as to which Pagan path or mythology they are drawn to, based on who they meet or what they read. Mistakes and false starts may be made until they are relatively comfortable within a particular spirituality. Someone once said that Paganism was a religion with homework, and I think I know what they meant: because it is not pre-packaged, you have to do some research to find what is suitable for you individually.

Why are you a Witch, Druid, Heathen, Shaman, Eclectic, Dianic, Ritual Magician, Eco-warrior, Quabbalist, Chaos Magician, Thelemite or any other of the myriad of choices?[3]

What is it that draws you towards one route rather than another? Does it align with some of your character traits or encourage you to change your mode of living? E.g. An accountant may be drawn towards a path with order and system, such as ceremonial magic. It may or may not be appropriate: whilst an ordered approach may seem more comfortable, a wilder approach such as Shamanism may open up other possibilities in their life. It should be an informed choice.

> *"Paganism rests on mythic foundations because of the use it makes of traditions, all of which embody mythological symbolism to a lesser or greater degree. As such these traditions offer substantive myths as building blocks for modern identity work, e.g. as a Celt, as a follower of the Northern way, as an Isian initiate and so on. Paganism can really do no other but to lean on myth in the kind of ways discussed – the resources of mythology being a very rich multicultural heritage from which to derive and develop new traditions based on seemingly ancient outlooks."*

(Ken Rees p. 29 in Harvey & Hardman, 1996)

Therefore, it follows which tradition you decide to follow could influence your future identity depending on your reading of its mythology.

How do you relate to the Gods & Goddesses?
Having chosen a path, one usually has to deal with its Gods and Goddesses. Is it necessary to identify and follow a specific deity? Some do not – they may refer to the overall *'nameless great spirit beyond the comprehension of mere humans.'* Having named Gods can provide handy shortcuts for some Pagans wishing to avoid lengthy explanations of their thinking on every occasion. I find it easier to say *'I was in touch with Thor'* rather than explain *'I was in touch with the righteous anger in my higher self.'* The latter is a quality that I individually associate with that red-bearded character that hits

enemies of the gods with a hammer. Others may see him differently. The ability of witches in the Netherlands to relate to a psychological entity and visible being at the same time was explored by Dr Léon van Gulik when he interviewed the late Merlin Sythove:

> *"I see the images of visualisation as an interface between my subjective world, and the objective divine world. I say 'objective' because I regard the divine-spiritual world, not as a purely fictitious world that only resides within itself, but I regard it as a really existing, real world. But of course, the images come from my subconscious, they come from things I've read, fairy tales and the like. Those images- of course, I realize that these are my constructions. – are as it were, a possibility and gateway for the Otherworld … In that sense, meditations are meant to silence the physical senses, while the visualisations   are a tool for the Otherworld to pass through."*

(Gulik, 2017 p.173)

Merlin talks about his meditations there but is not specific about whether they form part of a personal ritual. Meditation is a valuable adjunct to many religious paths, although it can be a worthwhile secular tool. Some groups of Pagans specifically come together to share what are either termed 'pathworkings' or 'creative visualisations.' These may often be completely independent of any particular Pagan orientation, so they are helpful to many mixed groups of Pagans. I wrote a practical book about the process. (Jennings, P. 2019)

I once met a man who said that he was a Pagan but did not have any named gods. He certainly didn't perform any rituals or try to do magic. He said that he was an enthusiastic fell-runner, and when clutching a tree on a hillside, exhausted and out of breath, he was closest to his Deity or whatever it was. I believe that was a very valid way for him to live his Pagan experience. Why should he have anything more complicated when this fulfilled his needs for a higher being?

> *"Neopaganism nevertheless puts a fundamental emphasis on ecology and on the environment. It advocates a sacred ecology that repudiates the Baconian ethic of human domination over nature and the capitalist outlook that views nature simply as a commodity or as a resource to be exploited. An ecological critique of capitalism and mechanistic philosophy goes back, of course, to the nineteenth century, but Neopagans reaffirm this critique and advocate a love for and a 'kinship' with nature. Neopaganism is thus conceived as a religious outlook that is 'nature venerating' (although rituals and prayers are usually addressed to the spirits or the mother goddess, perceived as anthropomorphic beings), and Adler concludes that all the Pagan traditions emphasize a 'reverence for nature' (Adler 1979, 23; Carpenter 1996, 63–4; Harris 1996)."*
>
> (Morris, 2006 p. 275)

Some gods and goddesses are seen as forces of nature. Their names may translate as 'waterfall' or 'cloud', so Pagans who say that they simply worship the forces of nature have a valid point. Within many modern Pagan rituals, there are invocations to 'the Elements.' These are usually Earth, Fire, Wind and Water, sometimes joined by 'Spirit.' Many other cultures have elemental lists of varying lengths and complexity.

If one thinks of the wind in the mundane world, it is a thing that nobody can see, but almost everybody believes in it. We can see its actions as leaves move across the ground, but not the force itself, similar to how some people believe in a God. Scientists may dazzle us with theories of variations in barometric pressure, but they remain that, just theories. I am happy to believe the meteorological theories. Still, until we

The Pagan Thinker

have the proof that has eluded them, I might as well believe in the Norse eagle Hræsvelgr (corpse-eater), sitting at the top of the world tree Yggdrassil causing the wind by flapping its wings, with the hawk Veðrfölnir (wind-bleached) perched between his eyes. It certainly makes a more picturesque story and more convincing to people with no knowledge (or belief) in science.

As a Heathen, I am happy to explore the Norse and Anglo Saxon mythology, learn lessons from it, enjoy the stories, and analyse their sources. I also identify very much with the Anglo-Saxon concept of a 'Web of the Wyrd' (Bates, 1983) where all parts of life are interconnected, and disturbance at one point causes ripples of consequences across it.

At my core, though I picture the characters in it as part of my 'higher self' or psyche, competing for attention and often in direct competition. The cartoon-like idea of a demon and angel sitting on my shoulders encouraging me to *'eat the cake' and 'don't eat the cake'* respectively appeals to me. Eating the cake usually wins! As a Pagan, I do not believe in 'sin', a construct of some other religions to ensure guilt from doing things against their moral code. However, I believe in 'right' and 'wrong.' In this case, it may be wrong for me to enjoy eating cake if I am overweight and diabetic, but right to enjoy the pleasures of life in moderation.

Incidentally, the concept of sin is a powerful one and can be hard to defy for a convert. It is also hard for some people of other religions to accept that we deny it, since their faith may rely heavily upon it: *"be a good follower and you will go to heaven, be sinful and go to hell"* seems to be the message. Although there are variations of the definition of sin between the world's major religions, within Christianity:

> *"The Bible uses many words for sin. Many are expressions that view sin as a failure or a "falling short" of a standard. In this sense, sin is a failure to keep*

God's law ("lawlessness," 1 John 3:4), a lack of God's righteousness (Rom.1:18), an absence of reverence for God (Rom. 1:18; Jude 15), a refusal to know (Eph. 4:18), and, most notably, a "coming short of the glory of God" (Rom. 3:23). Thus, sin is the quality of any human action that causes it to fail to glorify the Lord fully."

(Morgan, C. 2021)

One of the problems is that 'sin' has become associated with criminal acts, maybe due to it being, as the Christian pictures it, as *'failure to keep God's law.'* Inevitably, God's Law is not the same one adopted as national criminal justice statutes. Most Pagans believe it is wrong to kill each other and thieve. However, they may not go along with many other prohibitions issued by the more prominent world religions that are not seen as criminal acts in every country. E.g. many people over the legal age of consent have sexual relationships before getting married. That is recognised as 'normal' in many countries and so is not against the law. Some religions prohibit it though, because it violates their moral codes and is thus considered a sin. If a particular religion dominates a country, its politicians and leaders, it is likely that to have sex outside of marriage is against the law with severe penalties. This is where confusion can arise between sin and illegality. As Grieve puts it

"Neo-pagans consider guilt the opiate of the masses, a way by which organized religions manipulate the individual."

(Grieve, G., 1995 p.93)

In becoming a Pagan, one does not have some great moral authority to tell you what to do or not to do, so you need to decide your own standards, which we will explore in a later chapter. There is a sense within some Pagan traditions that some deities may punish us if we choose to do the wrong thing, but that is not a universally held belief. What does seem more common is that we are not craven to our gods: kneeling, demeaning ourselves and pleading is not a part of our regular practices, whilst thanking, remembering and honouring are.

Knowing yourself

The mythology you choose may have a connection with a feeling of 'belonging' to racial or tribal identification. Your God and Goddess may be simply called the Lord & Lady, but more often have complicated names, back-stories, attributes and relationships. They may seem very aware of you or entirely disinterested. They can have benign or uncaring, vengeful, peaceful, and many other characters, but all have a purpose. Depending on your circumstances, you will sometimes need to be closer to one Deity than another, yet not abandon others.

To do this, you need to know yourself in detail, something that some people never obtain in a lifetime of soul-searching therapy or intense experiences. Very few people entirely know themselves and how they would react in particular circumstances. We have all heard stories of the meek and mild person who unexpectedly goes into a highly violent frenzy against someone who attacks their child. Rarely would they predict this for themselves and may even be horrified by it afterwards. This also raises the issue that if we do not know ourselves, how can we understand others?

The famous magician, Israel Regardie, was a secretary to Aleister Crowley, a close confidante of Dion Fortune and connected to the Golden Dawn. He was an early proponent of the work of Freud, Jung and Reich.

> *"Legitimate esoteric orders have always been primarily intended to provide a context within which initiation may safely and effectively occur. As will be shown here, there are many parallels between initiation and forms of psychotherapy that take into account the spiritual dimensions of growth. Regardie even advised that the two should be considered as complementary*

The Pagan Thinker

*processes, and that initiation should always be
accompanied by some form of psychotherapy."*

(Monnastre, C. and Griffin, D., 1995)

As a trained counsellor and psychotherapist, I can concur with Regardie. The well-known witch and psychiatrist Dr Vivianne Crowley said, *"Jung's concept of archetypes accommodates readily the polytheistic worldview found in contemporary Paganism."* (Crowley, 2002 p.3) The book *Facing the Darkness* by Cat Treadwell (2013) is particularly useful as an approach to depression in Pagans who may have difficulties explaining themselves to some counsellors.

Some negative consequences of becoming a Pagan
Whilst there are many positive outcomes for someone adopting Paganism into their lives, have you considered some of the negative consequences and whether you could deal with them?

1. Being thought mad, bad or eccentric by less well-informed people.
2. Upsetting your family or friends by being open about it.
3. Prejudice in the workplace or community. (Illegal, but it still happens.)
4. Being frustrated because you cannot be open about it.
5. Finding it difficult to meet a partner because of your beliefs.
6. Having to adopt a new lifestyle that complements your beliefs.
7. No longer being sure what you should be doing or thinking.
8. Not fitting in with the general community.

There are no doubt many more reasons that you can think of for not becoming a Pagan. If there is any consolation, some very positive reasons may relate to how you respond to those negative aspects shown above. E.g. You don't have to care what people think of you in this new community, and you have already decided to adopt a new lifestyle. If a religion does not change you, then it is failing. Humans are usually risk and change-averse, so that it could get scary! It could cause you, like me, to completely change your career. E.g. A Pagan called Jenny Uzzell switched to becoming an undertaker![4] It could even result in a new appreciation or interest: some Pagans I have met have been led to a new understanding and involvement with art, music, poetry, astronomy, reading, craft, drama, writing or politics.

Crisis of Faith

"I've been a Wiccan for 13 years and have had several crises of faith, usually caused by a traumatic event that led me to question not the reality of Deity's existence, but whether or not Deity gave a damn about me, and whether I had the power to actually change anything in a universe so vast and complicated that seemingly random disaster could befall me just as easily as it could befall someone who believed in nothing."

(Sylvan, D., 2007)

Most spiritual paths have the concept of a 'Crisis of Faith' in which the follower has real doubts about their beliefs, in the existence of their Deity, their ability to conform to expected norms etc. Modern Paganism is not exempt from this experience, but it is exacerbated in not having proper support networks to deal with it. Whereas a Christian, Hindu or Muslim can go to a faith leader, priest, etc., Paganism has far fewer of these. For isolated solo Pagans not affiliated with any group, they have nowhere to discuss their issues and doubts other than on the internet. Those who do have some form of Elder, organiser, priest or priestess, are still less likely to have a relationship with them of the kind open to discussing personal doubts. In a small, localised group, the individual may feel alienated from the group in exposing their frailties. A local leader may not have any training or background experience to deal with such matters.

What's more, the more public, nationally known Pagan leaders, writers and activists may be hard to contact and inherently have issues that you should beware of before asking their assistance: I know because I am regarded as one! They may have books, courses or lectures to sell. They may be ill, or are probably insanely busy and may have fallen out with someone else in the Pagan community or even be suspicious of particular Pagan orientations, writings or groupings. In short, they may not be the unbiased source of advice you need!

The shock of having a spiritual experience may be more than a person can take. In which case, why pursue one?

> "When faced with the reality of the Gods and spirits, some Pagans revel in the confirmation of our magical worldview, despite the complications it brings. Others rationalize their experiences away in the hope they won't have to deal with spiritual beings with minds and wills of their own. Which group do you want to be in? Are you willing to do what's necessary to ensure that when the hopefully-metaphorical bullets start flying you respond the way you want to respond?"
>
> (Beckett, J. 2016)

The possible opposite of 'spiritual shock' is when one begins to doubt that gods even exist or are even aware of your existence. Other people's powerful arguments may bring it on, severe illness, witnessing disasters or the impending death of oneself or another. Coming to the end of a long-term relationship or job may prompt it when one tends to stand back and take stock of how you are doing. First, you will need to rely upon the previous relationship you had with your deities. If that sounds hard, it is, which is why you need to sort that out at an early stage of your chosen path. Next, you must consider whether the Gods would test you to beyond breaking point? Are they inherently benevolent to those who try their best 'to do the right thing', or do they have a cruel sense of humour regarding humans as playthings? If the latter, why should you bother with them? Unless, of course, you subscribe to the view that they are simply archetypes[5] of thought-forms from your mind?

That leads one on to another profound conundrum: what is a Pagan? Since nobody has the right to define what a Pagan is or tell you how to be a 'proper' one, the question is directed back to yourself. Only you can decide whether you are a Pagan or not, regardless of whether you meet other's expectations, look the part, know the theories or attend events. How do your beliefs affect your daily actions or attitudes? There is no point in having any spiritual path if it does not result in actions. Do you behave honourably? Do you feel the essence of a God or Goddess within you? What is in your heart and your head permits you to define yourself any way you want.

Chapter 3. Thinking about sacred places.

"Perhaps the central and distinctive feature of Paganism is the sacredness of the natural world, making it particularly appropriate for a society facing a human-created climate emergency which could lead to the extinction of many species, including ourselves. It could be said that the sacred text of Paganism is not a holy book but the natural world itself."

(Cush, D., 2019)

As well as visiting forests, moors, seashores and other wild places, many Pagans take great delight in seeing ancient stone circles such as Stonehenge, Avebury and the Rollrights. One hopes that they treat them respectively and not leave litter, light fires or damage old lichen colonies. Why they find such places appealing is a more complex question, to which you may have a unique answer.

"Contemplating and walking among the ancient stones evoked wonderment and appreciation that we had been privileged to experience them. This 'specialness' is linked

to ideas about the relationship of the distant past to the present and future, what it means to be human, and the process of identity-construction and self-improvement that spiritual tourists typically seek in their travels. This third hypothesis is confirmed by accounts such as those found on the internet and in Cope's idiosyncratic but profound The Modern Antiquarian."

(Cusack, C., 2020)

Involvement by Pagans within such sites can be seen as positive not just for themselves but the curators as well:

"We have offered an overview of how pagans perform their identities on the stage of Britain's heritage, from pilgrimage to Stonehenge at the winter solstice, to protesting against the destruction of archaeological material due to road-building or quarrying, and some expressions of heathen identity deploying archaeological visual cultures. We argue that these creative engagements with the past and re-enchantment practices should be of serious interest to archaeologists, heritage managers and other implicated parties, just as they are taken seriously by pagans themselves. Far from being inauthentic and separate from heritage discourse and management, such praxis is intrinsically linked to the situating of performance in these discourses."

(Blain & Wallis, 2008)

In contrast to a previous period when archaeologists ignored them, Pagans are now sometimes considered as appropriately interested parties at some sites. However, the relationship isn't always an easy one, as Rathouse explains:

"Decades of defamation, dismissal and sometimes discrimination left parts of the Pagan community with a disjointed and sometimes hostile range of interactions with 'establishment' organisations: on the

*one hand there has been a desire to maintain
anonymity thus avoiding discrimination, but on the
other there has been a desire to demand equal rights
with other religious and spiritual groups in order to
challenge discrimination. Within the archaeological
community and across the heritage sector there has
been concern that if all the demands coming from the
modern Pagan community were to be granted it
would become difficult for archaeologists and heritage
workers to fulfil their professional responsibilities and
perhaps even their ethical obligations."*

(Rathouse, W. 2021 p.1)

If you become interested in archaeological excavations related
to Paganism, you may have to think through your attitude
about digging up the remains of dead Pagan ancestors.
Should they be left undisturbed? Is it ethical to excavate,
examine and then rebury the remains? An organisation called
Honouring the Ancient Dead holds archaeologists to account.
Where and how should they be reburied? We are unlikely to
know the exact nature of their customs and beliefs. At present,
there are vast quantities of excavated bones lying in boxes in
museum archives with no plans to do anything but conserve
them for future generations to examine using new techniques.
How reasonable is this? It is no wonder that tensions exist
between the Pagans and Historians.

When land that is valued is threatened, some Pagans are
likely to be amongst those acting to save it. For example, a
particular road-building programme through sensitive sites
was instrumental in setting up a Pagan protest movement
known as the Dragon Network.

*"One campaign to which seemingly almost all Pagans
have allied themselves is the call to conserve and
preserve Britain's prehistoric monuments or 'sacred'
sites'. One common, perhaps universal, Pagan*

*explanation for why these places are sacred is
precisely that they are repositories of earth energy
and somehow vital for the well being of the land. As yet
campaigning centres around the prosaic tactics of
letter-writing, litter-picking and lobbying, but we
may yet see magical action centred around the
invocation of the dragon."*

(Lecher, 2004)

When Pagans tried to take part in the physical on-site
protests, they were not always understood or welcomed by the
Eco-Warriors that lived there all the time. Some protestors
(such as the Dongas Tribe[6]) had even set up their own tribal
religion.

*"The tactics of the protesters were to add so much to
the cost of building a road, that future projects would
become economically unviable: they lost each   battle
so as to win the war. But when road-building was finally
abandoned by the then-Conservative government, they
also quelled the very force that had given dragon-
raising its urgency and impetus and Eco-Paganism its
identity. By the time of the last major road protests in
1996, the Dragon Environmental Group had started to
become over-stretched; and with the demise of road-
building the organisation went into decline"*

(Lecher, 2004 p.194)

Since then, the movement has dissipated, with some Pagans
becoming directly physically involved in protests with others'
background support. More recently, many have become
involved in the Extinction Rebellion (X.R.) movement.
Whatever place you adopt as a sacred space, think about how
you can pay it back for letting you be there. Janet & Colin
Bord, who explored a significant number of secret places and
were interested in the idea of ley energy lines, concluded that:

"Mankind must quickly rediscover the needs of the planet and unselfishly try to fulfil them. Our mother earth has been e harmony. Our mother earth has been exploited for far too long, and no organism can live for ever without nourishment. The nurture we give will be to our mutual benefit, and the resulting interaction between men and earth, whereby the earth currents will again be available for mankind's use, must produce a much-needed harmony. This is the only way we on planet earth can not only survive, but flourish and develop."

(Bord, J&C 1976 p. 216)

Many Pagans worldwide have long been conscious of environmental issues, and many have united to sign 'green' statements.

"There is a presumption among many Pagans that Paganism is and always has been a "green" religion. In fact, it has been called "the Green Party at prayer." But Paganism, like every religion, is a complex mixture of concepts that can be used to either rationalize environmental neglect or encourage ecological harmony. Rather than characterizing Paganism, or any other religion, as "green" or "not green," we might rather speak about the "greening of religions," an ongoing, never-to-be-complete process. In this way, we can understand the history of contemporary Paganism as a "greening," one that is still going on, and 'A Pagan Community Statement on the Environment', as one small but valuable part of that process."

(Halstead, J. 2015)

Does celebrating Pagan ceremonies outside make a difference?

If asked, the average Pagan is likely to answer *'yes'* and maybe qualify that by adding *'because we are a nature religion, and so should be close to it.'* The sometimes unpalatable truth of the matter is that a large proportion of the Pagan population rarely celebrates rituals outdoors. The reasons they give are varied:

> I am afraid of being spotted by the public and harassed or reported to the police.
> I live in a built-up urban area with little access to unoccupied natural spaces.
> I lack the mobility to reach a natural space.
> Parks and recreation grounds are closed at night, and I am nervous about venturing out alone in case of attack. The few open spaces available are full of anglers, dog walkers, cyclists, and the like. Unfortunately, they are frequently spoilt with litter as well.
> I may venture out in summer, but it is too cold and wet at present.
> There seems to be little point when it is only me doing a solitary ritual. I may as well use my garden or the altar I have set up in my home.
> We haven't got any stone circles or similar unique places in my area.

I am not denigrating the people who use these excuses: I may have even used some of them myself at times. I am trying to highlight what Pagans say about being a nature religion and what they do, maybe two different things. I do not think as a spiritual path we are particularly hypocritical, and some of the reasons given are sometimes very genuine. But, of course, if you do not believe that Paganism is a collection of nature religions, it doesn't matter. If, however you feel guilty about being what is sometimes termed 'an armchair Pagan' reading about it in the comfort of your own home, communicating only via the internet, safe and dry by a cosy fire, think about your options.

Creating Sacred Space

You do not have to celebrate at night. A group of people sitting in a circle in the park is unlikely to raise much attention. If it does, you have a right to follow whatever religion you like as long as it does not break the law or frighten others, so minimise waving knives around or lighting fires. If you haven't got your own transport, maybe a bus is available during the day, or you can share a car or taxi with friends. If the area is strewn with litter, why not make a litter pick part of your ritual? You may even gain some kudos with the authorities!
(Headline: *Evil Pagans clean up beauty spot!*)

If you are convinced that you should be 'one with nature', shouldn't that include all of it, including wind, rain and snow? You may not have a sacred place in your area, but that doesn't stop you from creating one. If the Gods are all-pervasive, isn't everywhere sacred, including the litter-strewn clearing? I live in East Anglia, which has very few rocky outcrops, so no stone to make circles, dolmen, tombs etc. We haven't even got any hill figures such as the white horses or men that decorate hillsides elsewhere. Yet look on an old large scale Ordnance Survey map, and the area is covered in burial mounds with the occasional cursus thrown in for good measure. There are only one or two stone circles in the whole of the region, but that did not stop our ancestors from building wood henges at Arminghall, Holme-next-the-Sea and possibly other locations. They didn't fail to be Pagans just because they had not got a stone circle.

Sometimes a secluded garden can be the best place for a celebration. You can alter it to your needs and erect altars and statues if you wish. You could even physically incorporate the elements into your cardinal directions: wind chimes or weather vane for the wind, barbeque or a lantern for fire, a pond or birdbath for water and a flower bed or compost heap for the earth. (I will deal with the subject of The Elements separately.) I even heard of several witches incorporating round stone 'patios' into their gardens to mark permanent circles. If you bless your garden and call the gods, wights, genius loci elves etc., to protect it, shouldn't it be just as sacred as a stone circle?

I also have met Pagans who take a particular delight in gardening and connect with nature, fertility, seasons of growth and decay whilst doing it. Some produce herbs that they need for their healing remedies, and more than one plants seedlings and harvests them according to moon phases, something that many people still carry out regardless of their religion. It dates back to at least the 1st-century writing of the Roman Pliny the Elder.

Using ancient sacred sites

One must also ask whether using a location recognised of Pagan origins (such as a stone circle, burial mound) increases a ritual's validity? Is there any sense of cultural misappropriation? Maybe there is a more significant reason: to enable ancestor worship or to make some connection with them. Reverence for ancestors is an important component of many Pagan spiritual paths: for better or worse, they make us who we are today, and without them, we would not exist. Cheaply available DNA tests and ancestor tracing genealogy computer programmes are now readily available. Having a sense of where you originated from and who your ancestors are important to many people, not just Pagans. Having an interest in history, I found researching my family tree and finding my geographic roots a fascinating and absorbing activity.

In a paper concerned with the re-enchantment of both ancient sacred sites and the Pagans who visit them, Ben Birchall asserted

> "We have seen that Prehistoric sites are archetypal of landscape and nature and are therefore central to Neo-

The Pagan Thinker

Pagan spirituality. Therefore, I call for Prehistoric landscapes to return to the foreground in Pagan studies (as it was in the late 1990s and early 2000s) as it is essential to understanding Neo-Pagan beliefs."

(Birchall, B. 2021 p.27)

Theories about ancient sacred sites

Most stone circles were created thousands of years ago by the Pagan ancestors of some people living in the U.K. today. According to the latest research, in the U.K., they started around 3000 BCE or even earlier in the Orkneys and spread southward through Scotland, Wales, and England. We have no way of knowing what religions they were following then. Theories about the worship of a Mother Goddess etc., are just that until archaeologists can provide proof. Those theories may be well acquainted with that ancient historical get-out clause of labelling anything they could not identify as a 'ritual space!.' However, Luthaneal Adams does make a valid case for Pagan use of ancient sacred spaces:

"In the U.K., a lot of Pagans visit the many stone circles and earthworks that are scattered across our countryside. While there, we may just seek to connect with the place, or we may perform rituals. We know that the religion of the people who built the stone circles was not the same as ours and that we may never really know what their beliefs and practices were, but the site is still sacred to us because we recognise that these people probably had beliefs that were at least similar to ours, honouring spirits of the land and nature, so there is still a kind of kinship there. By being in these places and performing our own rituals, we're a part of the spiritual tradition of the site, and though we may do things a little differently and use different words, we are still giving the same reverence to the site and the spirits that reside there."

(Adams, N. 2021)

Some popular written and television sources are only too ready to serve up exciting tales of archaeological discoveries and conclude with cast-iron certainty with what it all means. With his experience of frequently being called upon to comment, Prof Ron Hutton lamented:

> *"By contrast, a proposal for a programme or serial on a historical or archaeological subject which tells the viewers or readers what is known and what the options are, and then invites them to choose between them, is unlikely to get commissioned."*
>
> (Hutton, 2013 p.400)

If we cannot identify that we are worshipping in the same way, is it inappropriate to do so? After all, it would not be appropriate to set up a Pagan ritual in a mosque or church. Surely it would be better to leave circles as fascinating places to view and set up our own sacred spaces just as they did. Furthermore, the members of Native indigenous spiritual traditions frequently feel strongly about cultural misappropriation by non-members of their communities. E.g. First Nation American spirit catchers used out of context and incorrectly in the West.

Creating new sacred spaces
Most paths of Paganism have an idea of concentrating rituals into a specific space, both physical and psychological and separating the 'other' world from the mundane. Surprisingly to many (including Pagans of other approaches), not all of them are circular. The historical sources of Heathenism inform us that a rectangular Vé (sacred space) was usual. The four of five elements usually invoked by most other Pagans seemed to have been restricted to two, ice and fire. So the standard form of sacred space is not the only one permissible. There is no reason why anyone has to follow historic example unless it has modern value. I would suggest thinking about why sacred space is essential and what form should it take? What

purpose does it serve to a modern Pagan? This quote from an Australian (where the cycle of the year is the opposite of the Northern hemisphere) may suggest some ideas:

> *"Employing Jackson and Henrie's typology of sacred space, we can see that modern Wicca falls into the mystico-religious category—where a site is perceived as sacred because God and humans are in direct contact. Once within the sacred circle of the witches, tine imagination can transport those inside into the limitless possibilities of an imaginary or 'fantasy' world. In his 'Feast of Fools', Christian theologian Harvey Cox applauded the virtues of fantasy, not simply because fantasy enables escape from lhe humdrum world of everyday life, but because it can be used as a device for creating alternative realities. (Cox, 1970)"*

(Hume, L., 1998)

At least one UK Pagan community has circumvented some of these issues and created the new Sentry Circle in North Yorkshire. The Odinist Fellowship bought an old de-consecrated chapel to make the first modern Heathen temple in Newark, Nottinghamshire. Odinshof and the Olgar Trust bought a Kent woodland where they could hold rituals and co-exist with nature. Also, a new woodhenge was set up by Moonhenge. In the USA, the Circle Sanctuary was legally set up in Wisconsin by Selena Fox as a Wiccan church, retreat and nature reserve. Other initiatives have followed it. Obviously, these are all collective efforts of groups of people working towards a common purpose and not open to all. Still, they may point the way for the future, since to a Pagan, all land is theoretically sacred.

Most of us tend to anchor our relationship with the land locally. So it is good to know that many area-specific esoteric books have been published for many U.K. areas. They often reflect long hours of research by their authors. E.g. in my native East Anglia, apart from my writing, there are excellent information books by Val Thomas (2020), Nigel Pennick (1995 + others), Terry Johnson (1996) and Nigel Pearson (2015 + others). That is a lot of Pagan writers for one English region. Still, it is not a complete list. The same applies to many other areas as well. Such books are likely to fast-track you into getting to know some fascinating information about the area in which you live. Reading Pagan writers may not be the only way to inspire yourself. Let me finish this chapter by quoting Adrian Cooper, who found his enchantment with others of mixed faiths in the mountains around the world:

> *"None of these people simply sat or stood beside a mountain and waited to become inspired. Rather, they developed a form of active dialogue with the realities around them. Many of them drew upon all their physical senses as they learned to find the full power of those contemplative moments. They considered carefully what they were seeing. They listened. They breathed in the distinctive mountain air. They thoughtfully ran their finger-tips across differing surfaces of rock, tree-bark, moss, lichen, stream beds, ice, snow and the dust of mountain paths. They tasted the spray of waterfalls, or dry, crisp Air on their tongues. Consequently, their prayers and meditations were rarely, if ever, one-dimensional spiritual experiences."*
>
> (Cooper, A. 1997 p. 287)

Chapter 4. Thinking about creating a circle

Regardless of where you intend to celebrate a ritual, (Indoors or outdoors) and whatever path you follow (except some awkward Heathens like me), you will likely want to create a circle.

Intent

Being a grumpy old Pagan, I am frequently annoyed, but one thing that is bound to upset me is a lack of declared 'Intent' either before or during a ritual. By that, I mean, what is the ritual for? Is it so we can look 'witchy' and display our best robes and jewellery? Is it to send healing to someone or someplace? Is it to honour particular Gods and Goddesses and remember a specific season, full moon, Sabbat etc.? Or maybe it is to work some specific magical act. In which case, you will need a clear intention for that.

> *"The first reason to set an intention is so that you get what you actually want. However you believe magic works, you want to be sure you are communicating your desires to the source of your power very clearly."*
> (Haseman, M. 2018)

I don't mind which, but decide beforehand, please! If the ritual has no firm intention, we waste our time and effort and live up to the idiotic image of the eccentric hippie's label that some of the public wants to give us.

Marking out the circle

Whether the circle is for a solo rite or a large group, its principles are similar. It will be familiar in form to many Pagan ideologies to be almost the expected norm. By now, you will hopefully have learnt to expect to question the 'norm', so here goes:

Why do we have to mark out a particular space? Indeed, isn't all the world sacred? The reasons that most people have told me are as follows:

A] To concentrate efforts on a focussed point.
B] To form a barrier against entities not wanted in the space.
C] A circle makes everyone equal – nobody is in a higher position.
D] Historical descriptions of gatherings of witches are always in a circle.
E] To make a portal between this world and the next.
F] *"It's traditional, and we've always done it like that!"*
(Sometimes added to by *'stop trouble making Jennings!'*)

A witch called Michelle Gruben advised:

> *"There all kinds of factors that can interfere with ritual magick: Distractions from the mundane world, the contrary wills of others, chaotic entities that feed off the Witch's efforts, just to name a few. Casting a circle is one way to shut out disruptive influences and stay focused on the work. Magickal trance can be a psychically vulnerable state, so many Witches cast the circle with psychic protection in mind.*

Just as important as the circle's outer barrier is its inner one. Magickal energy—like all energy that we know about—tends to bounce around and scatter off into the Universe. Motion is its natural habit. The whole point of ritual is to concentrate some of that energy temporarily, for a purpose. A circle allows you to gather more energy up and hold onto it longer. If your work involves the evocation of spirits or deities, a well-built circle offers them a cozy place to land for the duration of the rite."

(Gruben, M 2017)

When marking out the appropriate sized circle (with a sword, incense, chanting or simply walking), it is usual to move clockwise. If asked why, most Pagans will answer, *'that is deosilwise, i.e. the direction the sun goes around.'* I guess that the opposite (widdershins) would be correct for our friends from the Southern hemisphere, but since this book is about the U.K., European and American Paganism, we can move on. You may like to consider why following the course of the sun is important, though? Certainly, it is a natural phenomenon observed by our earliest ancestors, so that may be why it is considered 'right?' It should be pointed out that many Pagans will add a phrase *'As above, so below'* indicating that the barrier stretches under and above the ground forming a sphere, rather than just a circle. This would certainly seem to make sense, especially for reasons A-E above.

Suppose the circle is the reason [E], *'to make a portal between this world and the next'*. In that case, it may justify some other common actions: creating or linking 'Other' worldliness can be aided by blocking out all distractions from the outside. Drums, chants or music stop us from hearing background noises and may form a hypnotic beat that links into particular brain wave patterns. Using incense or perfumes will mask other scents. Dance may disorientate us from our sense of equilibrium, and linking hands will stimulate our sense of touch and belonging. The contrast of bright fires or lights with dramatic darkness and shadows will enhance our visual experience, as will ritual robes, masks, magical paraphernalia or nudity. Thus, all five senses can be stimulated within a ritual setting.

Calling Quarters

The next part of the usual process is to 'call quarters', which varies according to the path and tastes of those performing it. The first quarter called is usually to the East, which if one is following the journey of the sun paradigm would make sense because that is where it rises. The invocations are made in turn clockwise (deosilwise) East, South, West, and North. While Druids may say, 'Let there be peace in the East, ' Wiccans are more likely to say 'Watchtowers of the East, ' *etc. – bless our circle with your (East) air, (South) fire (West), water (North) earth.* They may also make the sign of a pentagram in the Air, with their pointed finger, a wand or an athame knife.

Pagans may also add a particular deity name associated with each of the cardinal directions or Elements mentioned.

Many Pagans at this stage will set lights at each of the quarters to mark them. Then, at the end of the ritual, they will extinguish them. This will frequently be done with candles. Indoors it can be acceptable (apart from the possibility of catching fire to clothes or furniture), but outdoors they are likely to be blown out by the wind. Inevitably some have obtained lanterns to contain their candles in safe, draft-free enclosures.

I once introduced a new young Pagan at a pub moot. The group were discussing which colour candles they chose for each of the quarters: *'Green for the earth in the North'* said one. *'I like red for the fire in the South'* offered another. *'No, I prefer yellow in the South for the flames,'* argued someone else. The newcomer whispered nervously to me, *"Why do they use candles in this day and age?* From the mouths of babes came the question that made the most commonsense! Fortunately, nobody insisted that their tradition had been handed down for hundreds of years and specified strictly which colours should be used. I would have quickly informed them that coloured candles were a mainly 20th-century invention! Use colours that mean something personally to you, I guess, is the rule.

Others provide battery-powered lanterns, hurricane lamps, blazing brands etc., instead of candles. So which of these do you think the most suitable in your situation? More profoundly, do you intend to do it at all? Nobody says you have to, and surely people can remember where the quarters were called. Of course, they add a certain ambience but are rarely bright enough to read out written words in the dark.

The Altar
An altar may be a sturdy table or a cloth on the ground. It is usually placed in the centre of a circle but generally pointing North. A quick survey of contacts confirmed an online source[7]: most Pagans set altars pointing North, occasionally East but felt that there were no set rules.

The words
That last point is an important one to ponder by itself: do you script the ritual for everyone and email it in advance, or make them all memorise it? That is not so bad if the same form is used each time, but off-putting if you end up having to learn new 'lines' for every celebration. I have even seen some Pagans downloading the scripts to their Tablets to magnify the text to a size they can read, which is backlit so that they can see it in the dark. *'No sense in having technology if you do not use it'* was one comment. The choice is yours, or you could just extemporise whatever words felt appropriate *'in the moment and from the heart'* as one Pagan put it. Some groups use a combination of methods so that the ritual is not

dominated by people intent on 'keeping their place' on flapping paper sheets. Nevertheless, it is undoubtedly essential to think about what the ceremony all means and experience it as a participant, instead of simply being an observer 'watching the experts' and trying to keep up.

One issue in re-constructionist[8] paths is whether to use the language initially associated with it, e.g. Greek, Latin, Old Norse, Celtic, Old English, etc. Once again, this must be a personal choice: it would seem arrogant to expect everyone at a ritual to understand the language. Do you avoid using it altogether (on the basis that the Gods will be glad to listen and understand anyone willing to talk to them), or do you recite a few passages (such as a poem) in original language sparingly, with a subsequent modern interpretation? Then you must consider whether the meaning of the ancient text is appropriate for a current ritual context? Does it talk of slaves, subjugated women, slaughtering nations or being beholden to a lord and master? Will it be understood in the same terms today?

Elements

Invariably at any modern Pagan ritual I have attended or read about (except some Heathen rites), 'the Elements' are invoked.' They are sometimes explicitly used in some forms of magic as well.

"Working magick with the elements helps to connect us to the tangibly present natural powers in our physical world, whilst at the same time we are returning to the building blocks of magick by rooting our feet in the material world. Since Empedocles formalized the system in ancient Greece in the 5th century BCE, the four elements have become an integral part of the Western Esoteric Tradition – passing from ancient Greek magick, through the Qabalah, & Grimoire Traditions into modern derivative traditions of ceremonial magick and Paganism….. In mastering the four

elements within & without we master ourselves, bringing the external forces of the natural world & the internal forces of our existence into harmony."

(Rankine & D'este, 2008)

Usually, Air is invoked in the East, Fire in the South, Water in the West and Earth in the North. Sometimes 'Spirit' is invoked in the middle of the circle, bringing the total to five. Only the top point in the North corresponds to any of the cardinal points for those who mark a five-pointed pentagram star in their circle. The practice of welcoming Elements to sacred space is so universal within Western Paganism as to remain generally unexplained or queried. Yet, it isn't relatively as straightforward as one might assume. Some take a radical stance akin to the Gaia theory[9] of the Earth being a living organism:

> *"The Earth is not an abstraction--a dead "rock" hurtling through space--but a living being. The elemental beings, who are intimately, intrinsically connected to the living Earth and to the living human race, suffer from our indifference, egoism, and ignorance of life, but they have much to teach us and patiently await our attention. Know your environment!"*
>
> (Massei, K. 2017)

Modern science does not support the classical elements concept as the material basis of the physical world. Ask a scientist, and they will say that the Atomic Theory suggests that everything is made of chemical elements, which can be found in the Periodic Table. New ones are found, but some are hard to maintain in a stable state without reacting to their surroundings. The periodic table of elements is a diagram of the chemical elements, ordered by their atomic number, electron configuration, and recurring chemical properties with metals to the left and non -metals to the right. These are only chemical elements, whereas occultists, alchemists etc., have referred to natural forces of nature as elements as well.

How many elements?
This is open to question, so consider a few alternatives:

Two elements: My personal version of the Heathen tradition only has two elements, Fire & Ice, that meet in the great void Ginnugagap creating the nine worlds. However, fire needs air to burn, and ice needs water and a firm surface such as earth on which to form, so the two incorporate the others.

Four elements: To the four elements already described, some modern Pagan sources add Spirit or even trees/wood as a 5th. Aether /quintessence/ spirit was not initially assigned as an element but has been incorporated by many people. It does mean that one can make a correspondence with the 5 points of the Pentagram.

Five elements: The system of five elements are found in Vedas, especially Ayurveda, the Pancha Mahabhuta, or "five great elements", of Hinduism are bhūmi (earth), ap or Jala (water), Tejas or Agni (fire), Marut, Vayu or Pavan (air or wind) and Vyom or Shunya (space or zero) or Akash (aether or void). These are sometimes used as parts of yoga and meditation practices.

Six elements: Sharma[10] makes a speculative model of six elements: Earth, Water, Air, Space (Void), and Fire (Energy) are the five elements that everyone has heard of, plus Energy as the primary Element, from which the other four parts are generated. Separate from this, scientifically, there was a need for six biogenic elements to create life on Earth.[11]

Eight elements: Fire, Water, Earth, Air, Nature, Ice, Light, Darkness. Unfortunately, the eight-element system seems to be more a set of rule parameters within a large group of fantasy role-playing games. It does not seem to have much historical precedent, so use it at your peril!

You should ask yourself which set of Elements you intend to use in personal rituals? Do you see a need to invoke Elements at all? Do you want to develop your own set of Elements and correspondences that are intrinsically linked to your beliefs, path, geographic area, racial origins etc.?

Elementals

I include some notes on Elementals as well since they seem to be frequently confused with Elements, and as you will see, there are some connections:

An 'Elemental' is a mythic being described in occult and alchemical works from around the time of the European Renaissance and particularly elaborated in the 16th-century works of Paracelsus. From that perspective, there are four Elemental categories: gnomes, undines, sylphs, and salamanders. These correspond to earth, water, air and fire. The Renaissance idea was that Elementals were beings existing within specific alchemical elements.

Animist Jaq D. Hawkins *wrote, "I feel some form of spiritual essence in everything."* (Hawkins, 2018 p. 11), but not all Pagans are animists.

Within magic and the occult, generally, an Elemental is a personified force of nature with associated powers associated with their home's particular Element. In *'De Occulta Philosophia'*, published in 1531-33, several decades before the publication of Paracelsus' *'Philosophia Magna'*, Agrippa also wrote of four classes of spirits corresponding to the four elements. However, he did not give unique names for the types.

Paracelsus: (Philippus Aureolus Theophrastus Bombastus von Hohenheim, 1493-1541 CE) 16th-century alchemical work *'Liber de Nymphis, sylphis, pygmaeis et salamandris et de caeteris spiritibus'* gave us the following table:

Correct name (translated)	Alternate name (Latin)	Element in which it lives
Nymph	Undina (undine)	Water (West)
Sylph	Sylvestris (wild man)	Air (East)
Pygmy	Gnomus (gnome)	Earth (North)
Salamander	Vulcanus	Fire (South)

Paracelsus regarded them not as spirits but as beings between creatures and spirits, generally invisible to humankind but having physical and commonly humanoid bodies, eating, sleeping, and wearing clothes like humans. Paracelsus said that undines are similar to humans in size, while sylphs are rougher, coarser, longer, and more robust. Gnomes are short, while salamanders are long, narrow, and lean.

The Elementals are said to move through their elements as human beings move through the Air. Gnomes, for example, can move through rocks, walls, and soil. Sylphs are the closest to humans in his conception because they move through the air like we do, while in a fire, they burn, drown in water, and get stuck in the earth. Paracelsus states that each one stays healthy in its particular "chaos", as he terms it, but dies in the others.

If, as Paracelsus said, one Element dies within another, that must have consequences for mixing them in magic. Whilst air assists fire, pouring water or earth on it puts the fire out. People performing Pagan rituals invoke all four Elements:

The Pagan Thinker

maybe assigning each one a cardinal point of direction keeps them apart? When I asked several practitioners why they gathered the Elements, the usual reply was along the lines *of 'all my work derives from nature, so all parts of it should be present.'* Some sources suggest that Elementals are ruled by higher spirits such as devas or archangels (which in modern witchcraft are called Lords of the Watchtowers, the Guardians, or the Mighty Ones). Generally, elementals are looked upon as benevolent creatures that maintain natural harmony. You may agree or disagree with that!

If you are into astrology, you will be familiar with astrological signs being classed by Element:
Fire: Salamanders (Aries, Leo, Sagittarius)
Earth: Gnomes (Taurus, Virgo, Capricorn)
Air: Sylphs (Gemini, Libra, Aquarius)
Water: Undines (Cancer, Scorpio, Pisces)

Some Pagans believe that most natural areas have Elementals present. Some make a point to acknowledge them alongside gods and goddesses. You may come across the term 'wight' used mainly by Heathens. Some believe that wight is another name for an Elemental, whilst others draw a comparison with the 'light elves' of Norse mythology. Some people (especially some imaginative New Age websites!) include all sorts of beings into this category, from water babies to unicorns.[12]

You may choose to invite Elementals to your sacred space in addition to or instead of invoking the Elements. That has to be down to personal choice, and the vital point to remember is that you have options, which are not necessarily the same as what everybody else has chosen.
Using Elemental magic
There is a branch of magic in which 'Elementals' are created as servitors to do magical work for their magician. I do not intend to go into the processes here but needed to make

readers aware that these are very different from natural Elementals and should not be confused with them. They are sometimes also known as a 'fetch' or 'fylga' or even a 'thought-form.' I regard them as a detachable extension of a part of oneself. It is a very personal process. To create an effective house guardian, for example, one needs to harness your negative aspects to develop a successful guardian, e.g. suspicion, aggression, manipulation, and positive aspects such as loyalty and focus. It would be best if you warned them about visitors you want to welcome and release thought forms when you move on or no longer require them.

Cakes and Ale

Another frequently seen feature of many Pagan rituals is known as 'cakes and ale', even if the constituents are 'bread and wine.' I once knew of a coven with written rules, including one that specified Jaffa Cakes[13] would be on the altar for every ritual. Why shouldn't they legislate for their personal preferences?

Usually, the food and drink are blessed then passed around the circle for sharing. At the end of the rite, some food and drink are left at the site for the magical consumption of entities who have attended. Eating and drinking is also a way for human participants to 'ground themselves' before re-entering the mundane world, which is why it is left until the end of the ritual before closing the circle.

Sharing food and drink is a custom to show fellowship between many religious groups and cultures, so it is not specifically a Pagan act. The Reclaiming ritual festivals in the USA specifically ban alcohol due to considerations for recovering alcohol users and use fruit juice or other soft drinks. If you are a vegetarian, be aware that many Heathen rituals include meat consumption, following recorded practice in Iceland.

Some sizeable group rituals leave the eating and drinking to the end, or even after the circle's closure. That means participants can choose how long they stay for what turns into an informal party. Since everyone brings food and drink to these, one can expect at least some vegetarian options. You should decide whether divorcing the feasting part of the ritual to an 'add on' afterwards is appropriate to you?

I have known a few cases of the hosts providing all the food and drink. If all Pagans are equal, is this a fair expectation even if they offer? Should there be a donations box or subscription instead? It should be enough that someone provides a space and clears up afterwards, so is it fair for them to fund it as well? Or, is it a case of them wishing to 'control' the event? – *'We hosted it, so we get to say who is allowed in and what happens.'* This is how unwanted power differentials within a group can sometimes start. Group dynamics can be a minefield, so carefully choose which role you wish to play in advance if possible.

Closing own
Most practitioners will express the importance of closing down a circle:

> Saying thank you and farewell to all entities welcomed there and the participants. Earthing yourself to switch you back to mundane mode before jumping into a car to drive home.
> Undoing the magical connection (generally done by reversing the opening procedure) so that it doesn't become an open-house with a welcome mat to attract any passing spirits, desirable or not.

Some people keep a magical diary to record their experiences. This is best done as soon as possible – the detail will have faded by tomorrow. However, if you have a tradition that keeps a Book of Shadows amended (whether in pen and ink or keyboard and hard drive), you will need to finish the process there as well.

Once again, these are all choices, but the responsibility is with you alone if you choose not to make them.

Chapter 5. Thinking about the movers and shakers.

Many Pagans are suspicious about any form of leader or organisation, and one can understand why. Raven Kaldera eloquently summed up an issue for those coming into Paganism from other religions:

> *"After childhoods full of being told what they could or could not believe, many converts were so reactive to anything remotely seeming like a religious authority or doctrine that most Pagan groups fell back on 'if it works for you, do it', with no thought of creating a standard for future group practice."*

(Kaldera, 2012)

Of course, some groups of Pagans do find regular structures useful, especially Gardnerian and Alexandrian witches who have some set rituals, progressive degrees and High Priests and Priestesses. However, even within that structure, many of them will come up with new ritual methods. Other organised groups such as Druid orders have similar opening and closing ceremonies but alter the middle of their rituals at each celebration. Many other Pagans write or extemporise individual rituals for every occasion. Unless the duty of creating the ritual is rotated around members of a group, the writer will (however unwillingly) become seen as a leader by the others. We then have what may be termed as the 'bottom rung' of the ladder of movers and shakers within the modern Pagan community. There are many of them, busily working within their communities, often without any concern for the broader national picture.

> *"With influences as diverse as ancient mystery religions, shamanism and indigenous spirituality, 19th-century occultism, and the anti-authoritarian ethos of the 1960s counterculture, many Pagan communities today feature a priesthood that is unpaid, relatively easy to enter, and collaborative in its leadership style. Few, if any, groups concentrate authority and leadership in a small number of clergypersons who minister to a large community of laypersons. Instead, Pagan communities typically will ordain many - if not most or all - active and committed members to positions of ritual, educational, and/or organizational leadership."*

(Patheos.com, 2021)

The term 'ordain' is rarely used within U.K. Paganism: certainly, individuals may gain positions and titles through their group's general recognition. In initiatory paths, a particular grade may have to be attained as a prerequisite. Many Pagans will also recognise that we are all our own priest or priestess and do not need any intermediary between the gods and us. This is particularly important if one is mainly a solitary Pagan with no regular group. It means that you are solely responsible for all aspects of your spiritual practice and any contacts with the outside world. The words of C.S. Lewis seem particularly apt: *"Of all the bad men, religious bad men are the worst."* [14]

The Cherry Hill Seminary, a significant provider of Pagan courses in the USA, defined a list of five traits that they thought each Pagan leader should display: 1. Pay attention 2. Be flexible 3. Show appreciation 4. Take a holistic perspective, and 5. Combine openness, transparency, and trust. (McKay-Riddell, V. 2021) Of course, some of these 'movers and shakers' become well known. Like me, they take on positions of responsibility, write books, talk to the media, found websites, run events, give talks etc.

> *"Based on an engagement with the contemporary Pagan community extending about twenty years I would suggest that leadership is built in a manner similar to Lewellen's (1992:84) model for tribal or band leadership in which leadership is not conferred from one leader to another but rather dies with the outgoing leader and is then built up by the new leader through charisma and respect. Such community leaders may even be better able to shape opinion within the community than those who have leadership passed on to them. However, they have seldom been as didactic as clergy in established 'world' religions as adherents are generally keen to make their own decisions and authoritarian behaviour tends to alienate the kind of free-thinking counter-cultural individualists who tend to be drawn to Paganism."*
>
> (Rathouse, W. 2021 p.8)

Despite my ambition to be Supreme Dictator of the World and take the title 'Grand Purple Octopus, Guardian of the 9th Crystal Abyss', I was perfect for the job! ☺

As far as I know, there are no direct equivalents of the training organisation Cherry Hill Seminary in the U.K. or Europe. However, some organisations such as the OBOD & BDO Druid orders offer correspondence courses for their particular paths and membership.

Sooner or later, some of these local leaders get together with others to facilitate something larger. It could be a camp, conference or networking organisation such as a moot. Moots are mainly informal meetings of a range of Pagans and learning from each other. They may also hire speakers from outside the immediate community or even run an outing to an event or sacred place. They are often held regularly in a pub but may also occur in cafes, halls, or homes. They are great places to discuss varying practices, learn new information and make local contacts.

These local leaders may be democratically elected, but most often are simply activists wanting to get something going in their area. They are unlikely to have had much training in whatever they intend to do unless it is from an exterior body such as their regular work. Little has been written about Pagan leadership (except people bitching about them!), although honourable mention must go to Knight & Ellwood, who edited an anthology of thirty writers. (Knight & Ellwood, 2016)

How would you be as a Pagan leader?
You may consider being some sort of Pagan leader, either now or in the future? It needs a certain amount of ego to put yourself out there, but too bigger ego has been a stumbling block for some in the past.:

> *"As John Beckett stresses, in the end, "leaders are servants." Leaders serve those whom they lead, providing them with spiritual experiences and practical direction, sometimes at their own expense. "Good leaders do that work," concludes Beckett,*
> *"because they want to serve the Gods, their groups, the Pagan community, and the world at large."*

(Titus, T., 2016)

In a modern era, when we no longer make sacrifices of humans or animals, is being a leader and sacrificing time and effort an appropriate alternative to other charitable work? The type of Pagans that this work attracts in the USA was addressed in Gwendolyn Reece's paper. An abstract from it reads:

> *"This quantitative study, based on data from a large-scale national survey of Pagans, Witches and Heathens in the United States, compares Pagan leaders and clergy to those who do not hold a formal leadership position in a group. This statistical snapshot includes demographics, characteristics of leaders as Pagans, religious practices, and participation in the larger Pagan communities. Pagan leaders are older, more educated, and have higher household incomes than non-leaders. Although there are more female than male leaders, males are statistically overrepresented in leadership. Leadership is almost all voluntary, and emphasize commitment to Paganism. Leaders are more likely to have been formally initiated, have more years of experience in Paganism, and rank themselves as more advanced than non-leaders. They exhibit expertise typically associated with clergy in mainstream religions, and they participate in specialized magickal practices at higher rates than non-leaders. Leaders and clergy are not only more involved in their groups in which they have formal leadership, but also participate in activities as part of the larger "Pagan community" at a higher degree of frequency and take advantage of opportunities and resources in the broader Pagan community more than non-leaders."*

(Reece, G., 2017)

I do find it sad that in a religious path with a goddess and feminist ideals, that men still seem to end up in the majority as leaders. While many strong women are involved in Paganism, many seem to leave leadership to an 'alpha male. 'There is no 'glass ceiling' as there may be in business, but women need to take a more significant role. Although this survey was for the USA, I suspect the same would be found in the U.K. Wiccan paths tend to be more likely to be female-led than others, possibly because of their role within covens.

Sadly, as soon as some of these leaders venture a head above the parapet, it gets bitten by some rival wannabe or critic. Some burn out from the amount of time and sometimes money they have to commit in their unpaid free time. Others flourish and create ventures that live on long after their initial set up, supported by other Pagans who appreciate their efforts. We should care about this process, even if we are not directly involved in it ourselves. It affects the Pagan community as a whole: some of these local leaders represent their regions in national organisations, such as Druid orders, Witchcraft and Heathen groups, and in the U.K., the Pagan Federation, OBOD and Children of Artemis. It is only by these groups' efforts that progress has been made with recognition by governments, changes in the law, attitudes of the media and national events such as large-scale conferences.

Some leaders cope well, and others do not. Some find that nobody wants to take over roles that they are no longer able to carry out, and it is always down to the same overworked band of volunteers. That is not a situation unique to Paganism: the average volunteer in most organisations only lasts for about three years. (Konieczny, 2018) An American study (Scherer, Allen & Harp, 2016) concluded that having a spiritual life extended volunteer longevity. You will need to read the whole report to evaluate the reasons.

The big question for you is, how do you see yourself fitting into this network? Do you see yourself as part of it at all? Of course, you are unlikely to agree with everything they say or do, but do you view them as a positive asset to be supported in general or enjoy the benefits they bring, such as legal representation, but to act alone?

Part of this may be influenced by whether you are naturally sociable or prefer your own company. There is nothing wrong with either of those viewpoints, but they are relevant. So how self-confident are you with your personal beliefs and relationship with deities? Do you need the support of others to reassure you that you are not some deluded mad eccentric, or have you the attitude *'to hell what others think!'* As a new Pagan, I went to one of the few conference events available at the time. It would not have mattered what the speakers were saying or how good the stalls, food and drink were. As somebody that until recently had not encountered any other Pagans, to sit in a hall with a few hundred of them was thrill enough. I wasn't mad after all, or if I was, there were plenty more like me. It is easy as an old-timer to forget what an emotional moment it can be for newcomers attending their first event. We should ensure that they feel welcome, even if we only smile and say 'hello' to people we do not recognise.

Chapter 6. Thinking about sources of information

You have probably previously been subject to lots of negative or inaccurate information about Paganism by other religions, the education system, your family, workmates and the media. It will take some time to take onboard alternative views about Paganism. If that first information you believed has been wrong all of your life so far, how can you be confident in judging that you do not get fooled again by these new and contrary facts?

In a study of American Pagan's[15] Laubach concluded that claims of psychic experiences and knowledge tended to be judged for integrity based upon the perceived authority of the informant, their social standing within the Pagan community, the narrative structure and whether they may have any self-interest in the outcome, such as direct or indirect monetary gain.

Just because it is written in a book doesn't make it accurate! There have been some accounts on the origins of modern witchcraft that were once widely accepted by academics and witches alike. They were later discredited by more serious research:

> "Another figure who has had tremendous importance for the Pagan revival is British Egyptologist Margaret Murray (1863–1963), who claimed that there had existed an ancient, Goddess-oriented form of witchcraft before the Christianisation of Europe, which was later demonized and persecuted by the church. While Murray has been largely discredited in recent decades, her books were widely read, and her ideas had a strong influence on the emergence of the Pagan movement. In a similar vein, Gardner claimed that his Wicca was a continuation of a witch cult that had survived in secret for   centuries, and which was ultimately derived from a presumably matriarchal, pre-Christian society."
>
> (Hedenborg-White, M. *Contemporary Paganism* in Lewis & Peterson, 2014 p.322)

Inevitably, earlier authors' information is still in existence, and these two examples have been copied as 'facts' into hundreds of other works before being discredited. Gardner himself quoted Murray as academic proof of his ideas, so the argument becomes circular. Some modern Pagans will not have read more contemporary explanations or may not believe them.

> "Contemporary British Witches are currently experiencing a radical shift in the ways they conceptualize, evidence, and rationalize their history. Until recently, practitioners claimed that contemporary practices could be traced back to pre-Christian times: formal groups of Witches (covens) had a continuous and unbroken religious tradition going back to antiquity. This position has recently been subjected to extensive critique which suggests a prevailing scepticism to the

*idea of continuity and an alignment with recent
interpretations from scholarly historians. However,
while the "inventions" of earlier writers are criticized,
Pagans continue to feel connected to the ancient
past by privileging less-specific ideas about rural
traditions and the primacy of experience rather than
explicitly historical arguments; the use of the past is a
continually creative and ongoing process. Therefore, it
is clear that dynamic ideas of what constitutes both the
content and context of history are central
concerns for practitioners today."*

(Cornish, H. 2009)

Volumes of accounts have been published about historical persecution and the execution of witches. You may or maybe not interested in what seems distant history now, depending upon your viewpoint. Inevitably the accounts of the war were written mainly by the 'victors' so are generally biased, even if they do contain important information. Assuming that the 'Burning Times' happened, in the same way, would be erroneous, as witch hunts depended upon many factors. The very name 'Burning Times' is a misnomer in England where convicted medieval witches were generally hanged. (The penalty was burning in Scotland.) The number 9 million is frequently bandied about and repeated from one book (and song[16]) to another to approximate the number of victims. Most experts (such as Briggs, 1996) say that this is a gross exaggeration, although, of course, a single one was too many.

Some of the most critical texts in Paganism are highly contentious: who wrote them, who contributed or influenced them, and how was the information obtained? Typical of this problem is '*The Book of Shadows',* started by Gerald Gardner, which influences Western witchcraft to this day. (Heselton, 2003 p.209-211) Similar problems face ancient texts important as sources to Pagans inherited in fragmentary form or in hard to translate archaic languages. E.g.the Middle Welsh 12th century *Mabinogion* (Guest,1997*)* and the 12th century Irish *The Táin (*Kinsella, 2002). Similarly, the accuracy of the Old Icelandic Norse texts '*Heimskringla'* (Sturlusson 1991) and '*The Prose Edda'* (Sturlusson,1995) of the 13th century are the subjects of concerns because Sturlusson is writing about things that happened or were believed to have occurred two or three centuries beforehand. These older texts' problems are that their details were transmitted orally for centuries before being written down and subsequently copied into later editions, often with mistakes.

Pagans also need to be aware of other subjects: history, psychology, natural sciences, ecology etc., to have a fully rounded experience and so as not to become obsessive over a single aspect of their life.

So how are you as an individual intending to sort the wheat from the chaff and try to verify information? Comparing varying sources, checking credentials and common sense are three suggestions, but if you find better ways, please enlighten us poor struggling authors since it is a recurring problem!

Books
If I were a publisher, I would take excellent care of my potential Pagan readership: they are notorious for purchasing and reading significant quantities of books which they hoard, putting a dragon guarding its treasure to shame. One of the most humorous but accurate pieces of advice I overheard was an old-timer saying to a newcomer expressing their desire to 'get into' Paganism was, "You'll need a bigger bookcase then!" However, one must remember that

> *"Paganisms do not, to a surface view, have 'sacred scriptures', and Pagans often point to different constructions of spirituality that do not privilege conventional 'texts'. Even though Wiccans, to mark an exception, may regard their 'Book of Shadows' as a*

The Pagan Thinker

form of sacred text—in theory hand-copied without change from the coven's Book of Shadows—more generally each Wiccan's book is personalised with at least some room for change or addition and most Wiccans of our acquaintance recognise that their practices are not ancient. For the majority of Pagans though, notably most Druids and Heathens, scripture is not part of religious discourse. For these Pagans, 'sacred texts' or 'scriptures' are associated (though not exclusively) with dogma and religious fundamentalism, something that Paganism, as new and developing religious movements, are keen to avoid."
(Blain & Wallis, 2004)

In recent years the advent of print-on-demand technology, Information Technology, more accessible self-publishing of books and ebooks has made it far more straightforward for anybody to write and self-publish a book. Without an editor, proofreader or lawyer, they may suffer in quality, but they are readily available, and you have to judge them on their merits.

'Rabbits can easily drive cars': Just because it is written in a book (this book) does not make it true! Self-published books are more lucrative for the author if they can sell sufficient quantities, but they tend to be hampered by poor distribution and marketing.

Having a known publisher does give some sort of seal of approval in that it has likely to have gone through some vetting processes and that someone else has confidence enough to spend money producing it. It may get better distribution (especially overseas) and have increased credibility. Some academics will not even notice a book unless a respectable publisher produces it. They will expect it to be appropriately referenced and possibly proceeded by peer-reviewing. They are likely to check out the academic status of the author.

A critique of some academic labelling.

You may assume that books and papers produced from academic sources would be more factual and accurate than those from the esoteric publishing houses or Pagan self-publishing. But, unfortunately, you may be sometimes mistaken in that belief!

> *"The variety of religious positions commonly grouped together under the heading contemporary Paganism permit no homogenous reading of that phenomenon. As recent research on contemporary forms of Paganism has flowered in recent years, emphasis has been given to the nuances and complexities of this kind of these new religious currents. For instance it is clear that contemporary Pagan currents, such as Wicca, Ásatrú, and Roman Paganism, tend to vary significantly between themselves on matters of theology, sociological profile, and political tendencies. While varieties in the social manifestations of given groups can be partly explained by diverging religious/ideological content, it also holds true that ideological formations will be determined in part by the society in which they emerge."*
>
> (Asprem, 2008)

I have been using the term 'modern Pagan' to categorise the group of spiritual paths and religions I am involved in within the U.K. and Europe. However, 'Contemporary Pagan' would fit the purpose equally. Unfortunately, academic views, papers, books and conferences about Paganism seem to be rarely of interest to most practising Pagans, with some notable high profile and honourable exceptions.[17]

One of the stumbling blocks seems to be the academic need to label a phenomenon and then define it. When many words such as 'magic' used within the field are seemingly undefinable, this creates a problem and is made worse by introducing arcane academic jargon seldom used in the mundane world. Given the additional changes in language and meaning that all languages undergo, confusion reigns!

E.g. the word 'glamour' was initially used to indicate someone using magic to imitate the appearance of someone else, often to have sex with their partner. There are numerous mythological tales of someone pretending to be the wife or husband of someone to seduce them into bed. Therefore, the term 'to put on a glamour' was initially offensive. In the mid-20th century, female film stars had their appearance altered with makeup, wigs, clothes, etc., to make them more appealing to the cinema-going public, who sometimes wanted to be 'glamorous' like them. It was seen by then as a positive thing. A few decades later, some photographers specialised in taking photographs of naked young ladies who were termed 'glamour models,' thus re-acquiring a seedy reputation. The term 'glamour' remains the same throughout but alters according to context, fashion and perception. The same is true of many terms used within the field of Paganism. I have not heard the term 'putting on a glamour' within the modern Pagan culture, but I have heard the term 'shape-shifting' used in a very similar way.

A failure of the academic community to move with the times in acknowledging the development of Paganism since the 1950s & 1960s has resulted in many Pagans finding their work out of touch, out of date, and hard to read. Maybe one of the reasons for this is that they feel academia is out of step with modern reality within the Pagan community. As Dr Joanne Pearson says:

> *"Despite their commonalities, Wicca, Paganism and Witchcraft are not synonymous; however, the common perception among scholars has been to treat these different entities as if they were one and the same. The growing popularity of these religions over the last three decades has seen the development of a variety of*

forms of Witchcraft and Paganism which have fanned out from classical Wicca."

(Dr. Joanne Pearson in Poole, Robert, 2003 p.188-203)

The practice of lumping all the varied Pagan paths together is the equivalent of lumping all the Christian congregations together: Roman Catholic, Church of England, Jehovah's Witness, Baptist, Mormon and Methodist presumed to all have the same beliefs and practices as Russian Orthodox and Charismatic Evangelical congregations.

> *"Much like the great majority of world religions, contemporary Paganism is an umbrella term comprising several different traditions which lack organizational or doctrinal coherence. Paganism can thus not be treated as a homogeneous religion."*

(Hedenborg-White, M., 2014)

Less than half of modern Pagans class themselves as Witches, yet this may be hard to see from many publications. Many Pagans combine an interest in science and do not find it incompatible with their beliefs. The secretive, anonymous nature of UK Paganism has changed to many people using real names and contact details and openly attending Pagan moots, rituals and conferences. The reluctance of academics to read and quote from the explosion of non-academic esoteric books is evident when reading their works' reference sections and bibliography.

Even when academics started investigating Paganism, the response by 'the academic establishment' was frequently ill-informed, hostile or dismissive. Professor Ronald Hutton, who has published and broadcast well-respected in-depth research on the subject:

> *"reactions to the news of my research project from fellow academics were often accompanied by a greater*

than usual sensation of distancing, disapproval or derision."

(Hutton, 2003,p.273)

Many of the old issues of the supposed unbroken craft history eschewed by Dr Margaret Murray (1933) and J.G. Frasier's (1833) erroneous work bear little relevance for many modern Pagans. Professor La Fontaine ably dispelled the furore and fear of the false Satanic Ritual Abuse scare spread to the UK by American evangelical organisations in her report to the U.K. Department of Health in 1994 (1998). As a result, a more significant proportion of Pagans are more open nowadays about their personal beliefs, and a high percentage are users of the internet and social media. Concentrated work with the media by organisations such as the Pagan Federation, OBOD, CoA CoG, Circle Sanctuary, Greencraft etc., has resulted in fewer sensational tabloid and tv stories and more factual content. However, it is a continuing struggle that needs to be addressed.

Some of the academics that interact with modern western Pagans are also Pagans themselves or sympathetic to them. This leads to unfair criticism of their work and views, along the lines of *'that they are too close to the subject to have an objective view.'* Why should they be judged to be less rigorous in their research methodology than others? I find this stance quite ridiculous: since when are historians (for example) discredited from commenting on history because of the 'bias' of them being historians? If I want to build a brick wall, I would prefer to be taught by a bricklayer than somebody who has watched a bricklayer or studied books on bricklaying!

Terminology

"Neopaganism is an umbrella term. Paganism classically refers to the polytheistic religion of the Greek civilisation and the Roman Empire before Christianity became the Roman world's official religion. Paganism (in its classical sense) and neopaganism (as its

postmodern revival) are a body of non authoritative beliefs that reject the separation of spirituality and materiality, and in various ways ascribe divinity to nature and the earth. Under this heading, there is a great diversity of religious movements and beliefs. Unlike Christianity, there is no orthodox dogma, hierarchy, or canonical scriptures. Neopaganism is in fact characterised by an anti-authoritarian and anarchist spirit – accepting a plurality of belief systems, practices or 'paths'."

(Bahnisch, 2001)

Another academic issue that seems unfair is using the term 'neo-pagan' to denote a difference between modern Pagans and those of antiquity. While I would be the first to admit that there is no continuous unbroken line of European Pagan practice stretching back into history (which others previously claimed), the same can be said of most religious paths. Modern Christian worship and organisation bear minimal resemblance to those persecuted Romanised Jews hiding their devotions in catacombs in the early centuries, although they have inspired it. Still, nobody seems to term a modern Church of England devotee as a 'Neo-christian', and I would imagine that they would find it offensive. They may also point out that religious' names as proper nouns should be capitalised, so the titles should be Christian, Rastafarian, Hindu, Pagan, etc. Not acknowledging them with a proper noun is discourteous. Not capitalising terms such as Pagan implies a value judgment that pagans, neo-pagans, or heathens are inferior or are not 'proper' religions. Who decides which ones are 'proper?' Guess! There should be consistency in naming religious movements. Therefore in this book, I use the term 'Pagan' to include the various spiritual paths practised in the U.K. and Europe of the modern and pre-Christian or pre-Islamic origins. This approach appears to be supported by York (2003 p.60) and others.

The Pagan Thinker

Please note that I am trying to deal with aspects of modern Paganism in the U.K. and parts of Europe. The term 'neoPagan' quoted in academic circles in the main is used to label those who claim to be Pagans now in the West and excluding continuing native Pagan traditions in Australia, Japan, Africa etc. Some North American sources have caused confusion, amending its meaning to designate feminist, goddess-centred paths and associated LGBT+ debates. See Gus diZerega (2021) for a detailed analysis of these separate issues that do not seem pertinent within the U.K. Pagan community. Neither is the 'New Age' with which Pagans are sometimes associated necessarily using Pagan principles: the followers frequently 'cherry-pick' elements from several belief systems, e.g. angels from Christianity, karma from Hinduism, singing bowls from Buddhism, and some Pagans (myself included) make derisory comments or jokes about New Age practices, especially their tendency to re-package and over-charge for what were often free elements of other religions. Nevertheless, we do not, on the whole, regard them as Pagans and object to being categorised together with them by academics.

The Census
Historically the U.K. Government Census did not ask any specific questions about spirituality. However, there was pressure from several of the 'minority' religions and awareness that Christianity was losing position rapidly, down to 59% from 72% a decade earlier. Some experts predict that the population's Christian share could dip below 50% in the 2021 Census, meaning that the U.K. could no longer claim to be a Christian country. An increasing number of participants notified, 'No religion.' The Census started to analyse data entered into the 'Other' tick box under Religions. In 2011 the resultant statistics were issued as following for England and Wales combined. Separate surveys are conducted in Scotland and Northern Ireland. The England & Wales Census is being undertaken in March 2021. This time it leaves religion as an

optional question. I understand it will also only be counting Pagan as a single category, without registering varieties such as 'Pagan – Druid' as before, so a detailed breakdown will not be available this time. It will be some time before results are published, and after the compilation of this book.

Here are the numbers for categories believed to be sub-sets of a total of **80,153** for the 'Pagan' category England and Wales in 2011. There were about another **10,000** Pagans counted within the separate Census for Wales and Scotland.

Animism:	541
Druid:	4,189
Heathen:	1,958
Occult:	502
Pagan:	56,620
Pantheism:	2,216
Reconstructionist:	251
Shamanism:	650
Thelemite:	184
Wicca:	11,766
Witchcraft:	1,276

Although this was almost double the figure of about 40,000 for a decade earlier, several authorities believed that numbers were under-reported. This was because some Pagans may have used other categories of: "Mixed Religion" (23,566), "Own Belief System" (1,949), or "Spiritual" (13,832). "Vodoun" (208), "Traditional African Religion" (588) and "New Age" (698) adherents. Technically speaking, Hinduism is a group of Pagan religions with multiple deities, but it is usually counted separately. Realistically the U.K. total (excluding Ireland) for all Pagan paths could be estimated at **100,000.** Although the USA does not have an equivalent to the UK Census, writers have frequently estimated from other sources that the Pagan population of the USA is between **1 – 1.2 million.**

It can be noticed that the Wicca / Witchcraft numbers are a relatively small percentage of the overall 80,000. This was believed by many Pagans to be caused by the opening up and literature of other orientations such as Druidry, Heathenism etc. Back in the 1970s, it was hard to obtain books on any form of Paganism. Those that could be bought (sometimes from under the counter!) tended to be about witchcraft, without mentioning the other options available.

It was also believed that there was some under-reporting because parents reported the wrong category for their children over 18 years old. They may not even be aware that their son or daughter is a Pagan.

The Web
Internet sites are notorious for publishing lies, recopied errors, deliberate errors, fake mythology and unproven 'facts.' With much less regulation than the content of books (themselves sometimes inaccurate), anyone can set up a website without much prior knowledge.

You can learn from websites that Pagans should only use particularly coloured candles at each of the cardinal points of a circle and that these associations *'go back to the mists of time',* which is often a suspect phrase. This is even though coloured candles were not generally available until the 20th century and that most tallow candles before that were a yellowy white. Yellow beeswax candles were prohibitively expensive for ordinary people. Similarly, you can find all sorts of inaccurate material about many other aspects of Paganism as well, but the internet remains a handy, cheap way of researching information.

General media, T.V., radio, films and newspapers
The makers of T.V. programmes, films and newspapers do not
have vast libraries of learned books at their disposal.
Inevitably, an underpaid, over-worked researcher on a
deadline will frequently use those unreliable websites we have
just discussed to get their information. Sometimes they will try
and find someone to talk to on the telephone but are unlikely
to check their facts either. Trying to find a Pagan of a
particular orientation in the geographic area the journalist is
interested in is not easy since they rarely advertise their
contact details. Even if they exist, they may not want to talk to
the press, and obtaining private contact details will usually be
difficult. (Why isn't there a 'Pagan' section in Yellow Pages?
☺) As an ex-National Media Officer for the Pagan Federation,
I can tell you that journalists do not want a Cornish Druid when
they asked for a Yorkshire Witch. Local newspapers and local
radio stations want local people to interview, not a national
spokesperson. I say this as someone who wrote a column for
local newspapers and presented a local radio show for about
twenty years.

Conferences & Lectures
Although there are no guarantees, the information given at
lectures and workshops at Pagan conferences, moots and
camps is likely to be reasonably factual. The reason is that the
organiser will be booking lecturers that they already know
personally, or by reputation. If something said seems
questionable, then there is always the option of asking a
question, something less available through other information
sources. One of the problems lecturers often face (including
myself) is that people are sometimes reticent to ask questions.
They fear they might be seen as silly for not knowing or
understanding the point made. In my view, there is no such
thing as a silly question. The chances are that the question
you ask is likely to be the same one that other audience
members would have liked to have asked themselves, so you
are doing them a favour.

The Pagan Thinker

Folklore and Traditions

> *"Our notions of 'folk music' and 'the pagan' are historically intertwined, sharing roots that go back to German romanticism and the idealism of Herder and Grimm. This odd symbiosis has bequeathed us the idea that folk music is something old and other, at odds with modernity and urban living. Most of us now live in towns or cities but folk music typically expresses a desire for the supposed rooted certainties of the countryside and a lost bucolic golden age . Clearly the popularity of both folk and Paganism says much about our contemporary and oft-commented yearning for an imagined, enchanted past."*
>
> (Letcher, A. 2015)

Pagans will sometimes try to get nearer to the past by looking at various folk traditions. These could be songs, stories or dances and traditional customs. As a folklorist, I find the field fascinating, and there are sometimes links between my Pagan beliefs and my enjoyment of folk traditions. I have been researching, performing and writing about them for 50 years now, presented a radio folk show for 20 years, performed solo and with bands as a singer and organised folk clubs and festivals.

Unfortunately, there is a common tendency by both authors and enthusiasts in labelling any custom or song that is old as being of 'Pagan origins.' E.g. Morris dancing does not appear in historical records until the 15th century, a time of fiercely controlling church authorities who sometimes funded it and would have probably had anyone associated with Pagan practices arrested. Yet still, the false 'fact' that Morris Dancing is a Pagan relic is frequently repeated. I would like it to be, but I do not believe it is.

> *"Given the extent to which modern-day pagans take as a truism that many of our folk customs have,*

unconsciously, retained relics of their heathen origins is traceable to the success of one man's major opus - Sir James George Frazer's The Golden Bough, a multi-volume work published in the 1890s.

'It is difficult to overrate the influence of The Golden Bough. It offered a   pattern which was immediately and attractively available; and it proceeded to dominate attitudes and thinking to a remarkable extent. The vegetation drama, ritual death and resurrection, the sacred tree, became accepted elements . . .' So observed Roy Judge in his study of the Jack-in-the-Green, also noting that the Frazerian influence was complex."

(Trubshaw, B., 2021)

'The Golden Bough' (Frazer, 1890) has indeed been the subject of many challenges since it was published but still has some valuable core material if one takes the accompanying theories with a pinch of salt.

Funnily enough, many customs (include Morris Dancing) have become Pagan activities more recently. There are now many Pagans involved with traditional dances, custom traditions (such as my involvements as the Cutty Wren Bearer for *Old Glory Molly*, Green Man for *East Suffolk Morris* and 'The Clever Doctor' in the *Magic Mummers* play, which was staffed entirely by members of *Chelmsford Pagan Moot*. Whilst the Green Man and Cutty Wren may connect us with old Pagan ideas, that does not mean that they have done so continuously through English history. However, I have sometimes found an incredible feeling of 'rightness' in carrying out these roles that are akin to when a ritual goes correctly, so I am ambivalent about the origins or current nature of some traditional folkloric customs.

Do you find such customs and songs, Pagan, in feel, even if not in origin, or do you feel it is just a colourful way to get drunk? Is it appropriate for Pagans and Heathens to adopt these practices as their own without any clear historical evidence of their origins? How about researching and thinking about the traditional songs, dances, and customs of your area, including those that have died out?

Symbols

In the same way that I have shown that words change meanings over time, so do some religious symbols. Sometimes they are deliberately hi-jacked in the way that the Klu Klux Klan adopted a blazing cross symbol, or the Nazis misused runes. In those cases, the misuse should not change the symbol's meaning, but it sometimes does. Thus, for example, there is still a reluctance to use runes in Germany. Of course, the Nazis also used the swastika symbol, but if you encounter it in other places, you will realise that it has a much older iconography used by Hindus as a 'hooked cross' emblem. The swastika continues to be used as a symbol of good luck and prosperity for Hindu, Buddhist and Jain cultures. You will even find it impressed upon some Anglo Saxon pottery as decoration.

The famous witchcraft five-pointed star symbol is known as the pentagram and also has a chequered history. When surrounded in a circle, it is known as a pentacle. The Sumerians used the symbol as a sign of the deity Ishtar in ancient Ur. The pentagram has continued to be used as a symbol to the Greeks, Pythagoreans, Jewish Jerusalem, The Church of Jesus Christ of Latter Day Saints, Bahai and is featured on the flags of Morocco and Ethiopia where it refers to the 'Five Pillars of Allah.' Inverted, it has been used as a sign of Satanists. With all that backlog of historical usage, it remains a general recognition sign of Pagans, regardless of whether they are Witches or not. It is usually believed to represent the five elements corresponding to five points of the human body, i.e. head, hands and feet. Interestingly, some Christians used it to represent 'the five wounds of Jesus', and in Masonic symbolism, the pentagram represents the 'five points of fellowship.'

The Mjollnir, better known as the Thorshammer, is a symbol adopted by many modern Heathens. They are found within archaeology for both Anglo Saxon and Viking Pagan cultures. The sign or the object is sometimes used to hallow ritual items. Many Heathens may use the Thorshammer sign even if they are mainly dedicated to another deity.

Many Druids widely adopt the Three Rays of Awen symbol as a metaphor for 'flowing inspiration', but many other interpretations are given.

The design of a simple labyrinth or maze is sometimes used by people, particularly trying to avoid utilising the above symbols with which they do not wish to identify. Some Shamen, Earth Mystery Questors and Eclectic Pagans are amongst those. Some use a symbolic 'tree of life' in the same way.

Many more symbols are associated with Paganism, including several related to Egyptian iconographies such as the ankh, scarab, or winged Horus. The paragraphs above just cover some of the main ones. Hopefully, by now, you will have caught onto the idea that they can all mean a variety of things to many different people. This all suggests that it is crucial to consider with which (if any) symbol do you associate yourself? It will rarely come without some historical baggage. It may also be misinterpreted by some members of the public if you wear it openly as a piece of jewellery or t-shirt design. Many will mistake a five-pointed pentacle for a six-pointed Star of David and assume that you are Jewish! Wearing a swastika will appear offensive to most people, and the rest will rarely be recognised outside of our community. Problems arise when people buy pendants such as pentagrams as fashion items without realising what they stand for. I remember an embarrassing encounter on a train when I wrongly assumed the person sitting opposite was a witch.

Specific jewellery is sometimes used to indicate the status of a person within a Pagan group. For example, some witches use particular symbols of their degree of initiation. Within some branches of Heathenry, a silver armband denotes a gothi or gytha (priest/priestess.)

The more profound question is 'why do we need symbols? Do we need to feel like part of some exclusive club? If the sign is purely for ourselves, why do we not wear it privately beneath our clothes? Are we displaying it to shock or impress other people or as a mark of dedication to a particular spiritual path? Wearing a piece of attractive jewellery may be pleasant, but what ideas do we wish to convey by it? Do we want to advertise our allegiance to a particular path? Why? Symbols are powerful tools used by advertisers, politicians and sport promotors as well as religions. No wonder the most popular of them have to be protected by copyright law.

Chapter 7. Thinking about Pagan Theology

A lack of theology?

> *"As I learned more about Paganism historically, I discovered almost a universal lack of theology, from ancient Greece and Rome to modern Brazilian African Diasporic traditions. What books were more like books of shadows, with lessons on how to do something or other, than philosophical treatises on the nature of Apollo or Iemanja. Such studies existed, but never as a major part of Paganism. Pagans' religious energies mostly went into ritual and practice."*
> (Gus diZerega, 2021)

I think I know how Gus feels! Theology is not a term that gets mentioned much within modern Pagan circles in the U.K. or elsewhere. General theology is a complex subject, full of obscure terminology and controversial theories. One popular definition of theology is *'the study of the nature of God and religious belief.'* As a dynamic movement that accepts no overall doctrine, holy books or hierarchy, surely modern intelligent and educated Pagans do not blindly believe in Gods and Goddesses without questioning what they are and how we should express our beliefs? Academics have questioned whether Pagans can even have a theology?

> *"Is there really such a thing as Pagan "theology," or is the term itself too embedded within an Abrahamic religious context? Should Pagan theology more accurately be described as praxology, or theories of Pagan praxis? What would Pagan praxology look like and how would it advance our understanding of religion?"*

(Call for papers for a meeting of American Academy of Religion)[18]

I understand that 'praxeology' means *'the deductive study of human action'* (Collins Dictionary), but 'praxology' is either an Americanisation or misspelling. Praxis itself is *'practice, as distinguished from theory'* or *'accepted practice or custom.'* If they can make sense of Paganism's multitudinous practices and customs, they would have achieved something that none of us inside the movement have ever done!

Just as we in Paganism have many paths and many individuals with their own distinct and unique sets of beliefs, it may be that every individual needs their own personalised theology since a single 'one size fits all' approach is only suitable for an orthodoxy, something that nearly all Pagans do actually agree about: they don't want one! Some of these ideas were explored, discussed and developed by Yvonne Aburrow. (2010) She went on to say how Pagan theologies would need to be descriptive rather than prescriptive and have a quality of existing in parallel with others that may be different in some details. There were also likely to be some mutual connections, which may be derived from ancient or current Pagan practices, without their sources becoming regarded as canonical, i.e. becoming a source of rules.

Gus Butler (2012) presented some labyrinthine essays, and I would advise that they are not for the layman of theology.

Kraemer (2012) and Kaldera (2012) are more accessible.
Discussing Pagan Theology, the Russian academic Stanislav
Panin concluded that:

> *"I believe that the emergence of Pagan Theology is not
> a matter of chance, but a necessary stage of
> development, both in the conceptualization of
> contemporary Paganism itself and in Pagan Studies at
> the same time. An emergence of Pagan Theology
> reflects tendencies that one have been observing in
> these groups for years and that is why we cannot
> describe it as artificial phenomenon. It looks like Pagan
> Theology as a specific research   programme has
> emerged in Great Britain and in the USA, and not
> without reasons. However, nowadays this concept
> achieves more popularity in other countries too, and I
> believe that it is reflecting the contemporary situation in
> the development of Paganism."*

(Panin, S. 2015)

Unitarian Universalists acknowledge the truths they find in
many religions, and some of them class themselves as Pagan
influenced. For example, a Unitarian called Victor Ashear
summarised his five great theological questions as:

*1. Who am I (spiritually or theologically)? What is the important
nature of human beings?*
*2. How do I know what I know? This has been called the
question of "epistemology" meaning the study of knowledge.*
*3. Who or what Is In charge? This is the question of
"cosmology" from Greek, meaning order, rulership, or world.*
*4. What is my purpose in life? Theologians know this as the
question of "soteriology" from the Greek meaning, deliverance,
or reintegration.*
*5. What does my death mean? Theologians call this the
question of "eschatology."*

(Ashear, V. 2018)

I think that we could all spend a lifetime trying to resolve these five theological questions for ourselves, and they seem not biased towards any particular faith, which is why I chose them. Nevertheless, it is worth looking at the URL provided in the Bibliography to find his detailed expansions upon these themes if you are particularly interested in them.

A personal reaction to the five questions.
Looking at the five questions, for myself, I believe that humans are marvellous sentient beings with enormous potential. However, we shouldn't be arrogant about it and subjugate the rest of the world to our will. I can only learn about this by engaging all five senses and not accepting 'facts' and the status quo blindly without challenging them and revising my thoughts in the light of experience.

As far as who or what is in charge, I do not know and accept that it would probably be too much for my puny brain to comprehend. I can observe that there seems to be some logic and pattern within the natural world, suggesting some design rather than pure accident and evolution. Therefore, my purpose should be to get the best out of life whilst fitting in with the nature of its creation, acting responsibly and honourably.

Death is the big mystery, and that is probably just as well: if I have made the most of my life, I will not have regrets about wasting my brief time on Earth. The only people who can say for sure what the afterlife and the 'Otherworld' are like are the dead, and they rarely seem to describe them, even in spiritualist seances. I will have good memories to take into eternity, of whatever that consists. Maybe I will be reunited with my ancestors and animal friends in the mythological world I identify with, even if that only occurs within my mind. My body will become recycled into a new life after being broken down by fire or decay. Since the scientists tell me that energy can only be transformed and not be destroyed, maybe the electrical impulses of my brain will continue in one shape or

The Pagan Thinker

form or even incorporate into future 'ancestral memories.' If I have done worthwhile things in my life, I will live on by my reputation, so it is essential to maintain it and leave a legacy of good work.

I have noticed that Pagans are just as likely to use euphemisms that avoid the words dead or death: 'passed over to the Summerlands[19]' or 'gone over the rainbow bridge' are just two of those expressions. Is it because death is still too painful to confront directly? Whether we call it the Elysian Fields (Greek) or Valhalla and any of the other Norse halls of the dead[20], the concepts seem ill-defined. This is unfortunate when most religious paths seem to offer a wonderful after-life. Other Western Pagan mythologies include Annwn (Welsh), Avalon (Arthurian), and Tír na nÓg (Irish), but there are many more.

As I said, these reflections are purely my thoughts and maybe profoundly wrong and inappropriate for anyone else to adopt. They may change in light of experience and better arguments. I have supplied them to give an 'aunt sally' to bounce opposing ideas off so that others can find their thoughts. How do yours differ?

Specialists

Adherents of other religious paths can rely upon dedicated specialists to think about such matters and instruct the right way of thinking. As independent, free thinkers without hierarchy, we are responsible for undertaking this task for ourselves. We can be influenced by what we hear or read, but ultimately the decision is ours alone. A possible reason for some Pagans avoiding questions of theology was suggested in an online discussion group:

> *"Honestly, Pagan theological conversations are just not as common as they should be. In part I believe this is because many Pagan religions are still trying to figure out what they are actually all about, and in their growing*

pains we see many of the tough questions seem to function as divisors as they further splinter these religions into various ideological camps. This leads to many choosing not to question the narrative of whatever camp they find themselves closest to in order to avoid being put in the position of being alone.

All of that said I do think that there a few foundational theological positions emerging in modern polytheism: the belief in many real gods, and the refusal to claim objective reductive knowledge of what real means in this setting. In other words, polytheists may find Animism, Platonism, and many other theological approaches useful in trying to relate to the gods we generally refuse to give in to the natural human tendency of reductionism in that we do not, as a rule, claim that they must be these things, or that they are just X, Y, or Z."

('IrreverentPriest', 2018 in r/pagan)

It is difficult to comment upon the term 'Pagan theology' since Paganism covers so many divergent (yet related) spiritual paths, and as Lord Salisbury once said, *"If you believe the theologians, then nothing is innocent."*[21] A Witch's thinking is likely to be very different from a Druid, Heathen, Shaman or general Pagan, so it is not easily possible to generalise.

"Ultimately, no universally observed ethical principles define the Pagan movement as a whole, although mythologically-derived notions of virtue and honor, the Wiccan Rede, the acceptance of magic as a tool for exercising spiritual power, and a balanced sense of the importance of caring for the environment are widely held values."[22]

These factors have made it challenging for the academic community to analyse Pagan theology because of its diversity and lack of the dogma associated with monotheistic religions.

In her study of Pagan theology, the well informed, retired Pagan Federation president Prudence Jones said:

> *"Pagan thought thus contains the religious world of European antiquity, it contains tribal religions worldwide, both ancient and modern, and it also contains Hinduism, Shinto and other sophisticated polytheistic faiths. It is the theology, the reflective thought, of this religious outlook that I am examining here, and I am skimming through the broad trends of ancient thought in order to put modern thought in context."*

(Jones, P., p14 in Harvey & Hardman, 1995)

Thinking about cruel gods

I have met Pagans and other people of different beliefs who had turned away from Christianity. Their common denominator was this: in a religion that declares that its God is all-powerful, created the world and everything in it, how is it that he/ she can appear so cruel? Innocent children killed and abused, populations wiped out by disasters, unending wars, tyrants, murderers, thieves and rapists, famine and disease: surely He could stop all that and care for his creation? One of the responses to Christian people who have had great hardship in their lives (such as the death of a child) has traditionally been 'God is testing your faith' although more latterly Pastors simply answer that 'no one knows.' Why should he do such a cruel thing? He is supposed to give us free will to choose whether I follow His ways, but can't he protect us?

> *"Sigmund Freud called religion an illusion humans invent to satisfy their security needs. To him, a benevolent, all-powerful God seemed incongruent with natural disasters and human evil."*

(Wright, R., 2007)

In some ways, the issues above seem nullified by the nature of Pagan beliefs: if a volcano is part of nature, we as Pagans of a nature religion should appreciate it as just that, without ascribing any malice to its destructive power. We cannot just love the beautiful parts of nature like cuddly animals and trees: we have to like poisonous snakes and earthquakes as well and see that they have an equal role to play in nature 'red in tooth and claw.'[23] We may enjoy watching both lions and zebras, but the lions will die of starvation if they do not eat some zebras. Whose side are you going to take? The lion presumably does not see killing a zebra as a 'good' or 'bad' act. Those are value judgements imposed by some humans. It would seem unnatural for us to ask our gods and goddesses to stop the laws of nature of which they are a part. Maybe if you hold to the idea of Lovelock's Gaia theory, when disaster strikes, it could be a sentient Earth ridding itself of a few human parasites?

Some of our Pagan mythologies portray the deities as having little interest in humanity: they are often too involved in their fighting, seduction and adventures. Sometimes they may notice a human and elevate one to a celestial lover or damn them with rape, death or punishment. It seems from some stories that we may only be for their occasional amusement or as the butt of cruel jokes and fates. How one interprets that in your relationship with the gods may depend on your attitude to the myths and personal character. An unlucky old Heathen friend of mine would simply look up to the sky and ask, "Why me?"

Many of the evils of the world are man-made, from deforestation to pollution. Most of these are ultimately caused by humans being greedy, wanting more money, power and an easy life. Yet humans and their conflicting character traits are part of nature, too: do we reject all humanity due to a minorities selfishness? As Pagans, we can try to persuade them to act differently, of course, in whichever creative ways we find within ourselves as the most effective. We can also strive to not being part of the problem by colluding with governments and businesses who behave badly. We are getting into the ethical issues, which will be tackled in the next chapter, but it also relates to those earlier thoughts of how we relate to our deities and which information and leaders can we trust? As I said in the introductory chapter, all the issues overlap and are interdependent.

Disorganised Religion

There is a problem in that some Pagans reject terms such as 'religion' to describe their beliefs, preferring other labels such as 'spiritual path' or 'way of life.' I honestly believe that this is more due to the general confusion between the word 'religion' and the description 'organised religion.' Religion means 'thinking about god(s)', which we all do in our individual ways. However, many Pagans fiercely reject anyone trying to organise them, get them to join a society, turn up on time or represent them. They fear that this may lead to some form of recognised orthodoxy. There are old but accurate jokes that say wherever three Pagans are gathered together, there will be five opinions and that Pagans are as easy to manage as herding sheep.

The Pagan Federation (of which I am a retired President) has had to meet this issue for years. They try to act as a networking organisation, negotiate with government and other institutions, promote Pagan rights, and facilitate activities across all the various paths, but often get damned by those outside it who do not understand its current role. I know that some Druidic and Witchcraft organisations have similar problems in that Druids and Witches will complain that *'they do not represent my individual views.'* My comment is, *'So don't join!'* However, such individuals may be grateful for what those organisations achieve (such as negotiations with the government, environmental actions, events, anti-defamation work, legal defence), all without offering them any practical or financial support. E.g. the official legal guidance on religious discrimination in the UK workplace was partly due to seven years of work by the P.F. It has been used successfully in at least two legal cases and sent a clear message to others considering discrimination. How do you now feel about supporting some of the efforts of the various Pagan organisations available? Progress has also been made in the USA, particularly the servicemen's rights to follow their spiritual paths and have a pentagram on their gravestones.

Diversity

Outside commentators have said that Pagans tend to work out things by doing rituals rather than by debate over the nature of their worship. I believe that is accurate for some adherents, but not all. We have lots of informal discussions around campfires, moots, internet forums, magazines etc., but these are rarely reported. A speaker at a conference, camp or moot may spark fierce debate. Still, it is unlikely to be recorded or even thought to be worthy of writing down since one opinion may be valued as equally as many others. This is just one of the outcomes of Pagans celebrating our diversity rather than finding it divisive. We learn from each other without having to get defensive about our own beliefs.

Many other Pagans practice solo, so they do not have these opportunities. They may even be content with holding Pagan beliefs but not taking much action related to them, just as some people are nominally Jewish, Muslim, Christian etc. but are not actively involved. Such people, including Pagans, may consequently be nearly invisible. The U.K. government census has revealed far more people describing themselves following Pagan paths such as Witchcraft, Druidry, Heathenism, Shamanism etc., than has ever been revealed by the membership of organisations and sales levels of specialist magazines and books. Would you be visible as a Pagan in surveys? Would you want to be, and why?

Academic views on Pagan theology

Much recent academic activity concerning Pagan theology takes as its starting point the influential book by the British religious studies scholar Michael York, *'Pagan Theology'* (2003) which is understandable. No single book in the intervening seventeen years has approached its depth or breadth of detail. However, it does suffer from generalising about a very diverse path (Witchcraft, Wicca, New Age, Druidry, Heathen, Shamanistic, Eclectic etc.) and contrasting it with indigenous Pagan spiritualities such as Australian Aborigines, First Nation American, African Tribal, Japanese Shintoism etc. Nevertheless, he does produce a worthwhile statement about this:

> *"In comparing classical and related pre-Christian paganisms with Christianity, we find that paganism includes (1) a number of both male and female gods (2) magical practice (3) emphasis on ritual efficacy, (4) corpospirituality, and (5) an understanding of gods and humans as codependent and related."*

(York, p.14)

I have written about the similarities and differences between modern European Pagan paths within my books (2002 & 2019) and do not wish to be pulled into the academic array of arguments about definitions or to examine the reconstructed beliefs of ancient Romans, Egyptians & Greeks. Nor am I concerned with modern Australian Aborigines, Voodoun practitioners or First Nation Americans and Canadians. I doubt that any of the individual members of those groups think identically. This brings about a fundamental problem for academia, which, by its nature, likes to define, categorise, and measure them. Within Paganism (and many other religions), it results in academia trying to categorise things that are too diverse to be associated together and attempting to define the undefinable.

Medieval ecclesiastics are now laughed at for arguing about how many angels you could get on a pinhead. From current evidence, the modern academic process of creating definitions could instead be accused of being at the stage of trying to define the meaning of a pinhead rather than analysing the essential principles and issues.

Finding our truths

A group of five Pagans may hold six differing opinions and be content to do so. Within Paganism, there are no agreed divine texts or over-arching authoritative leaders. Therefore, each Pagan has to find their personal truths and respect others' differences. They may do this by a combination of discussion, research and intuition. They may also change their (open) minds when confronted by a new viewpoint or data. Individuals of other religions may follow this same process but may find themselves censured by their leaders or community if they are perceived as too different or disrespectful. For Pagans, the difference is profound: the absence of hierarchy and divine literature results in them not usually being condemned for different beliefs by their community, however diverse they are from the perceived 'norm.'

It is a fact that many Pagans celebrate their diversity together and attend events that attract a variety of spiritual paths. They listen to each other's talks, read each other's literature and enjoy understanding another type of Pagan, despite being comfortable with remaining in a different grouping. They may even ask the others why their way is most attractive to them, without any disrespect or urge to 'convert' them. You overhear conversations that start, *"Ooh, a shaman! I've not met one before. Come and have a drink and tell us what you do and what it means!"*

Divisions

It is logical for some Pagans to form smaller organisations or internet groups to accommodate shared minority beliefs, or alternatively to operate as solo practitioners because they think that they are the only person in an area to feel as they do. They may also take that position because of a dislike or distrust of organisations in general. That sometimes happens in other religious denominations, where individuals choose to operate alone rather than join a mosque, temple, church etc.

If we compare Paganism to Islam and Christianity, there are some similar issues: Islam split into Sunni and Shia traditions. Christianity has subdivided ad infinitum into separate denominations with differing viewpoints around some central ideas. E.g. Catholic, Protestant, Mormon, Jehovahs Witness, Baptist, Methodist, Orthodox etc. Still, even within those congregations, individuals will frequently hold various interpretations of those views, sometimes in opposition to the religion's teachings. E.g. Surveys in the U.K. and the USA have found that high percentages of the populations know their star signs and regularly read their horoscopes, despite labelling themselves as Christians.[24] The Christian Bible explicitly forbids divination, sorcery and hidden arts (Deuteronomy 18:10-14) but the Pew Forum on Religion and Public Life stated that

> *"Many U.S. Christians – as well as the religiously unaffiliated – hold "New Age" beliefs, which include belief in reincarnation and astrology."*
>
> (Gecewicz, C., 2018)

The many schisms and followers separating into various congregations within Christianity (and to an extent in Islam, Hinduism etc. as well) are generally perceived as a negative thing from both within and outside of those faiths. On a smaller scale, modern Paganism has also split into many various factions. The difference is that most Pagans see this as appropriate and a positive move: they will focus on the shared beliefs and work together in rituals, camps, conferences, publishing etc.

There is a secretive strand of Witchcraft in Italy called Stregheria. A small number of adherents in the USA have made attempts to learn more about their tradition. Still, apparently, their respective practices are very different. How this relationship survives and develops is of interest to the limited number of people involved (possibly in the low hundreds). In contrast to more significant world religions, it is unlikely to involve schisms within Witchcraft. Most other Pagans or academics are unaware of this tradition, and it has a very low public profile. (Magliocco, S. 2021

Outsiders who understand the distinction between Druids, Heathens, Witches etc., may see co-operation between groups and individuals as a logical move. It must be acknowledged that the general public does not make such finite distinctions between individual strands within a faith: they tend to generalise them into Pagans, Christians, Muslims, Hindus etc. and regard any inter-denominational conflict as unworthy of spiritual people.

Chapter 8. Thinking about Moral Rules and Ethical Principles

No single religion or individual has a monopoly over doing good things. One of my favourite authors, the late humanist Terry Pratchett wrote: *"Goodness is about what you do, not what you pray to."*

Moral and Ethical Principles are not usually enshrined in law. However, they can be powerful in that one has to be seen to adhere to these 'unwritten rules' to be seen as a worthy member of a particular community. That community may be racial, political, religious, employment or even a specialist community that has set itself standards that may be higher than the general community's norm. E.g. Social workers, medical staff, police etc. To be seen to break those principles would possibly lead to sanctions or expulsion from that particular community.

> *"Absolute morality is the regulation of conduct in such a way that pain shall not be inflicted."*
>
> (Spencer, 1891)[25]

Yet Pagans do not seem to discuss ethics in any great detail. As Ian Jamison found:

> *"On the rare occasions when Pagan authors did write about ethics, it was uniformly articulated solely in a magical context ("You shouldn't put curses on people"), an approach frequently linked to the rather anodyne statement of ethics known as the Wiccan Rede, (the benevolent sounding, but rather impractical — "An it harm none, do what ye will"), sometimes combined with a vague sense of some kind of karmic repayment from the universe."*
>
> (Jameson, 2011)

Since not all Pagans are involved in magic, this seems rather short-sighted. Surely there should be standards which they or their community should adopt concerning all the other activities in which a Pagan may become involved? Additionally, the Wiccan Rede only technically applies to Wiccans, not the whole Pagan population, although they may choose to adopt it as well.

Some general moral principles (Source: Brown, 2020)
Treat Others the Way You Want to Be Treated
Speak The Truth/Do Not Lie.
Don't Spend What You Don't Have.
Keep Your Word.
Don't Take What Doesn't Belong To You

Some people may ask, "why not leave it to our conscience?" which is a reasonable question if one understands how conscience is usually constructed. I very much agree with the view given by Druid Emma Restall-Orr, in that conscience is such an integral part of us that we are not typically conscious of its origins :

> "*Nowadays behavioural psychologists speak of conscience as an inner source of doubt that is learned, developing through the positive and negative feedback of our actions, not least those of early childhood. So is our conscience often an eerie inner echo of our parents, and the religious, school and social authorities of our earliest years. As such, we have conceived a thousand ways to suffocate that little judge inside, drowning out the quiet voice by turning up the noise of life.*"
>
> (Restall-Orr, 2008)

Many people (Pagans or the general community) may intuitively find moral principles easy to acknowledge as valid. The devil is in the detail, though, and as Pagans, we may encounter problems living up to them completely. When personal relationships with partners, family or other Pagans go wrong, would we always treat them as we would like to be treated? That would mean not ostracising them, verbally or physically abusing them or even cursing them?

If we were assaulted, would we not respond physically and not leave it to some form of Karma to resolve? If they stole from us, would we not try to recover the goods or report them to the police? On a minor note, have you ever lent a book to someone who, despite reminders, failed to return it? That is stealing to, and reportedly rife within the esoteric community. Interestingly, libraries report that occult themed books are some of the most frequently stolen items.[26] Stealing doesn't always relate to objects: consider the author who copies ideas from other books without giving credit for their origins (which is why I like to reference quotations.) Alternatively, think about the pirated versions of music, films, literature or even tarot packs that steal royalties from the musician, film-maker and author. These are not victimless crimes.

If our partner was doing wrong to someone else, would we speak the truth and not lie to the police? If we promised to keep a secret by someone who later became an enemy, would we still keep our word not to get them into trouble? Is the notion of a white lie ever valid?

If we found a book or ritual article that we wanted, would we borrow money from another fund such as rent or utility bills to buy it? If, instead, we found that item lying in the street, would we keep it rather than handing it to the police?

> *"Perhaps the most important way to live morally is to trust your instincts or what you feel deep down is right. You can't always explain what causes you to feel a certain way, but in many cases, you can tell if something feels wrong. Be sure to avoid taking actions that make you feel uneasy."*
>
> (Brown, A., 2021)

None of us is perfect, and even when we believe in a principle, we still may fail to uphold it due to our human frailty. Also, some types of Pagan will have different codes that they support, which may change the response. For example, I am from a Heathen path, which does not include the 'An it harm none' principle. Therefore, I would have no hesitation in physically attacking someone who threatened me, my family or my home. I see this defence as a religious duty in that I should not give in to wrong-doers or fail to challenge them. However, we Heathens have an accentuated appreciation of keeping one's word and not telling lies, so I would be duty-bound to admit to the police that it was me who injured the burglar/ attacker/ rapist etc. and take the consequences, if any.

Many other Pagans have an absolute abhorrence of all violence and take comfort in their belief that 'karma' will result in a bad outcome for the aggressor later, either in their current life or in a future incarnation. (Sometimes labelled as 'the law of three-fold return and applying equally to good or bad actions.[27]) That outlook frequently requires the victim to believe in reincarnation and Karma, which certainly aren't universal beliefs within the Pagan world.

The idea of Karma is sometimes used loosely along the lines of 'what goes around comes around.' However, if one looks at its source, the truth is more complex.

> *"The word Karma is derived from the Sanskrit Kri, to do: all action is Karma. Technically this word also means the effects of actions. In connection with metaphysics, it sometimes means the effects, of which our past actions were the causes."*
>
> (Swami Vivekananda, 1998)

However, since the word Karma should be seen from a Hindu[28] and Buddhist context, it is inter-related with the idea of multiple reincarnations being experienced until complete enlightenment or Nirvana is achieved. So if you embrace the concept of Karma, it may imply that you are content to see someone run off with your money because they will ultimately have to pay for this action, either in this life or one of those to follow. Forgive my cynicism; I think most people, including Pagans, would pursue the thief and forcibly retrieve the money; I suppose this could be perceived as saving them from future Karmic retribution! As for being physically attacked, I certainly do not believe in the Christian style of the admonition of 'turn the other cheek!' The delivery of my equivalent of instant Viking Karma would be swift and violent. I would not apologise for the harm or feel guilty since my tradition does not include any prohibition against harming, just encouraging behaving honourably and being independent.

A set of *'Nine Noble Virtues'* has been adopted as a set of principles by several Odinist / Asatru / Heathen groups. John Yeowell (a.k.a. Stubba) (1991) possibly wrote it for the Odinic Rite in the U.K. sometime in the 1970s, but there are various other contested claimants, including John Gibbs-Bailey (aka Hoskuld). They were based upon values exhibited within the *Hávamál* and *Sigrdrífomál*. Heathens tend to place particular importance on making and keeping oaths, and the nine seem to angle much more towards being independent and taking responsibility for one's self:

Courage, Truth, Honour, Fidelity, Discipline, Hospitality, Industriousness, Self-reliance & Perseverance. There are some slight variations of words and order applied to these, but all bear the same sentiments. Whilst they sound a good set of standards to live an independent life by, Isaac Bonewits offered this critique:

> *"Now it's true that bravery can turn into foolhardiness, a concern for honor into overbearing pride, loyalty into creedism, racism and sexism, and so on. For that matter, self reliance can turn into isolationism- the belief that one has the right to do as one pleases regardless of any negative impact on families, clans, tribes, or nations. Fortunately, strong Asatru men tend to have strong Asatru women around them to let them know when they are getting carried away with themselves! But clearly these virtues, also shared by many mainstream American men, are appropriate for a Pagan boy or man to use in following a warrior path."*
> (Bonewits, 2005 p.87)

I would add that I see no reason why a Pagan girl or woman cannot follow a warrior path. I detailed several Viking female warriors recorded historically, and since then, archaeology has caught onto this idea and revised the gender assigned to some Viking warrior graves. (Jennings, 2018 p.171-172) Talking of warriors brings me onto this guide produced for the US Military: The '*Spiritual philosophy and practice of Wicca in the US Military*' states:

> *"Many traditions still keep to the 164 'Craft Laws' or 'Ordains' ('The Book of Shadows' by Lady Sheba lists these). These ancient Laws were written in 20th century and are probably more a romantic notion than actually being the ancient and sacred laws they are often portrayed to be. In fact, they were written by Gerald Gardner. He began writing what he called the*

The Pagan Thinker

'Ardanes' shortly after he established his first public coven. They were written in archaic language to give them the flavor of antiquity. Gardner modified and added to these Laws over the years to suit his own views and purposes. Additionally, the Ardanes reflect the very patriarchal worldview common at the time that they were written, and many contemporary women find some of them highly offensive. Most Traditional Craft covens retain them in their Coven Book of Shadows purely as an historical artifact. Most traditions adhere to more modern —Covenants of Sacred Law."
(Oringderff & Schaefer, 2007)

N.B The American term shown above, 'Traditional Craft' covens, indicate those of the Gardnerian or Alexandrian paths. In the UK, 'Traditional Craft' indicates those non-aligned covens in operation before Gardnerian witchcraft's advent in the 1950s. Lady Sheba is a well-known witch in the USA.

Sex within magic
A great deal of interest has naturally been expressed by those who have seen references to the use of sex within magic. I sometimes think that some of them may be people who rarely experience sex in any other ways, judging by their excitement and fixation on this seldom-used ritual method. For a start, it is only usually connected to witchcraft, and as has already been noted, witches only form a small percentage of the Pagan movement. Within those, solitary witches, i.e. those not in a coven, are by definition less able to use sex magic. It tends only to be a factor in Gardnerian, Alexandrian and Thelemic practices, although it does not preclude independent magicians from being influenced by them. The three main historical protagonists of sex magic were Aleister Crowley (Thelemic), Gerald Gardner (Gardnerian) and Kenneth Grant.[29] (Typhonian / OTO), who were influenced by the Hindu Tantric practices from India. This was either directly or indirectly via the Hermetic Order of the Golden Dawn and which had high validity and interest during their lifetimes. (Bogdan, H. 2006)

> *"It is therefore quite understandable why to Crowley and Gardner the idea of the individual's freedom was often synonymous with sexual liberty. The morals and ethics of Western society and Christianity were regarded as restraints and restrictions imposed upon the individual, and in order to progress spiritually one had to break free from bonds of the 'old' values. Often enough, the most explicit way of breaking free was to adopt a new antinomian[30] sexual morality, which in the case of Crowley was based on The Book of the Law. The supreme secrets of the O.T.O. in the form of sexual magic, and the Third-degree initiation ritual of Gardner's Witchcraft movement, can thus be interpreted as a way to challenge the morals of Western society and a means to break free from them."*
> (Bogdan, H. 2006 p. 239)

Some witches may still celebrate 'The Great Rite,' i.e. sex between a priest and priestess as part of a ritual to raise magical power. Frequently, this will be between existing life partners and not necessarily in front of other coven members. Others have changed the 'Great Rite' to a ceremonial form, symbolically plunging an athame blade into a chalice.

You may have to make moral decisions about all of this if you join one of the few groups celebrating the 'Great Rite' traditionally. You may also want to think about whether you are willing to practice witchcraft 'skyclad,' i.e. naked. Again, some groups who used to be skyclad now wear robes. Nakedness is not seen as necessarily being sexual within the Pagan community, and it has been mainly other religions that have decided that nakedness = sex. One must remember that Gerald Gardner met with his coven at Brickett's Wood, near a naturist camp and was a naturist himself. This is why I may emphasise asking questions about a group you are interested in joining in Chapter 8!

Rules

Setting accepted standards of behaviour of visitors to Pagan & Heathen events became the subject of an agreed code by a range of UK festival organisers, with some itemised details but summarised as:

> *"We are committed to providing a positive and trouble-free experience for all, regardless of gender, gender identity and expression, sexual orientation, disability, physical appearance, body size, race, ethnicity, age, theological perspective, or relationship status (polyamory, monogamy, singleness). We do not tolerate unacceptable behaviour in any form. Anyone violating these rules may be sanctioned or expelled from the group or event (as appropriate) [possibly without a refund] at our discretion."*

(Pagan And Heathen Symposium, 2015)

It has to be stressed that most people attending Pagan events are friendly, generous, non-judgemental and inoffensive. This code was set up to deal with the isolated individual who may not be so cordial. I guess if you do not think it fair, then you do not have to attend.

Ethical Codes

There is a crossover between moral principles and ethics, which numerous authors have sought to define. It seems generally agreed that Ethical Codes are far more likely to be written down than general moral principles. Bird & Winkelstein[31] identified four broad themes within the Ethical Codes of eight American organisations. The organisations were working mainly in the medical sphere. The themes were:

Autonomy (Confidentiality for individuals, not being biased in reporting their views)

Beneficence (Using the maximum skill and competence and placing the individual's wellbeing above other concerns)

Non- Beneficence (Not compromising an individual through incompetence)

Justice (Giving equal access to information, providing resources with a diversity of opinion and respecting intellectual property rights.)

Gracyck (2012) drew similar conclusions. Many professional work organisations publish such ethical codes. In some fields, it is hard to operate without signing up to one. E.g. To obtain insurance and recognition as a counsellor in the U.K., one must join an organisation such as the BACP. To enter, one must sign to agree to uphold its core ethical principles. Breaking these principles may result in membership being terminated. Sometimes the issues are complex and need to be discussed by a peer group committee since two ethical principles may clash. E.g. a person could be an illegal immigrant who is very ill and needs urgent medical attention. Their status excludes them from anything but emergency medicine, and notifying authorities will result in their expulsion from the country. If your ethical principles include always working to uphold the law and always giving medical assistance when needed, a conflict of principles may occur. Some social workers and health professionals frequently face such ethical dilemmas and have complex codes of practice and documented ethical frameworks to inform them. However, there are always some cases that fall outside the 'textbook' examples.

Principles

The Free Dictionary defines moral principles *as "the principles of right and wrong that are accepted by an individual or a social group."* As a general rule, morals are what we use to guide our actions. There are some moral principles that most people agree on and others that differ from group to group and person to person. Many people can follow moral principles by following laws.[32]

Principles tend to be based on personal values, which are not universal. For example:

> *"In other societies, personal freedom may be seen as less important than other things, such as observance of religious rules, or family loyalty or social cohesion. Different cultures use different criteria to make choices, presumably as a result of different circumstances and different traditions."*

> (Beckett, Maynard & Jordan, 2017)

The above quotation was for student social workers' guidance. One of the authors (Andrew Maynard) made a lasting impression on my thinking in the dynamic classes he facilitated at Anglia Ruskin University, Chelmsford. In forming our 'core values', we must deeply examine ourselves before letting them become enshrined as written principles.

Some Pagan organisations have a set of principles to which one has to sign up for membership. For example, the UK Pagan Federation originally had Three principles that all prospective members agreed to uphold. This code became a controversial issue since some genuine Pagans felt unhappy to agree with all of them, dependent on their individual views. Since then, the Three Principles have been incorporated into the Constitution, but membership is no longer dependant on them. However, some P.F. branches that became independent entities decided to keep them, including PF Scotland and P.F. International. There are slightly different versions of them in existence, but they can be summarised as:

1. Love for and Kinship with Nature. Reverence for the life force and its ever-renewing cycles of life and death.

2. A positive morality, in which the individual is responsible for the discovery and development of their true nature in harmony with the outer world and community. This is often expressed as "Do what you will, as long as it harms none".

3. Recognition of the Divine, which transcends gender, acknowledging both the female and male aspect of Deity.

Whilst these Three Principles may seem relatively innocuous, they engendered passionate debate and adjustment. Some people thought their individual paths were not based upon a nature religion, so they rejected number one. In my path of Heathenry, not much is said directly about reverence for nature within the ancient texts: maybe because the natural conditions that the Norse peoples lived in were frequently harsh and hostile. However, there are personalised forms of the sun, moon etc.

The wording of number two was hotly contested since it was felt that it was unduly influenced in the final sentence by Wiccan and Crowleyist thinking, summed up in a phrase adopted by many witches 'An it harm none.' It is probably derived from Dorien Valiente's *'Wiccan Rede'* that she produced for Gerald Gardner in 1964 and echoed a text by Aleister Crowley, by whom Gardner was influenced. Most wanted a 'do no harm' clause, but not worded that way, except some Heathens who felt like me that we have the right to do cursing and negative magic if attacked. Many agreed to a 'do not start harm' instruction as a moral position, although it was pointed out by many that someone can't live in a way that avoids all injury to others, e.g. walking over insects or plants etc. so it would be unrealistic and impossible to live by.

The third principle was not so hotly contested, except by those who simply saw their deities either as (a) a single goddess or (b) a single male god and single female goddess, from which all other gods and deities were seen as purely alternate aspects. The majority of modern Pagans tend to acknowledge a whole pantheon of gods and goddesses with different names and attributes, usually from a particular culture such as Celtic, Norse, Egyptian etc. They may also believe that there are other valid pantheons but prefer not to mix them with their own set without viewing them as competition. It should be noted that some Pagans do not acknowledge any named god or goddess and simply refer to a nebulous 'Great Spirit' or similar.

The diverse nature of Druidry has given its members a daunting task in translating the complex Celtic mythology into practical rules by which to live. As leading Druid Ross Nichols commented:

> *"Druid teachings are drawn from many sources. In reality, a good deal of this wisdom exists at an archetypal level, and can be accessed with proper training. That wisdom which is written down can be found in the Order's course, much of the writings of the authors mentioned in the Foreword, and in early Welsh and Irish texts, although these are often difficult to obtain or obscure to interpret. "*

(Nichols, R. 1991 p. 265)

General moral principles are likely to be less well defined and fluid than written rules and laws. They are more likely to be formed in individuals influenced by societal or religious influence, so they are more likely to change in the light of experience.

Ethics or moral philosophy is a branch of philosophy that "involves systematising, defending, and recommending concepts of right and wrong behaviour".

Laws

Laws are the system of rules that a particular country or community recognises as regulating its members' actions, which it may enforce by imposing penalties.

While many laws are based on moral principles, (e.g. murder), not every moral principle is a law. E.g. pre-marital sex (subject to age, country, gender etc.). Just because a dominant religious group decides that they have a rule based on their beliefs does not make it valid to those who do not share them. That can cause conflict, e.g. non-Muslims drinking alcohol in an Islamic country that prohibits it.

Where some <u>individual</u> Pagans may be at odds with U.K. law:
Partaking of drugs
Under-age drinking or smoking
The requirement of children to be schooled
Trespass on private areas that they consider should have free access.
Non - payment of taxes that they feel are being misused
Refusal to serve in armed forces if called to do so
Taking part in protests

Where some <u>individual</u> Pagans may be at odds with U.K. society without breaking laws:
Not being a Christian or agreeing with some aspects of Christianity
Sexual choices, e.g. homosexual, lesbian, polyamorous, bisexual.
Use of alternative or complementary healing methods.
Not living in fixed accommodation
Not having respect for 'the work ethic' and maintaining a regular job
Dressing differently, wearing hair in different styles or colours, tattoos, jewellery, crossdressing
Green politics & activism as an eco-warrior
Homeschooling or insisting the child is excluded from religious studies at school.
Believing that protecting the natural environment is more important than anything else.

Let me show a contrasting viewpoint: Emma Restall-Orr (aka Bobcat) is a leading Druid for whom I have the utmost respect and affection. She was Joint Chief of the *British Druid Order* and organises *Honouring the Ancient Dead*. (HAD) We have publicly discussed ethics and have opposing opinions on many issues. She concisely constructed a precis of much of what her thoughts were on which ethical principles Pagans should share in *'Living with honour: a Pagan Ethics* (2008). It is a book that I can thoroughly recommend as an antidote to this one.

> *"Perceiving all nature as sacred, retaining personal responsibility and autonomy within the community or web of nature, as Pagans we strive to live sufficiently aware of the currents and tides of our own soul, that we might open ourselves to sharing our intention and, wakefully, respectfully, connect with another (human, blackbird, beetle, buttercup, raindrop, storm, or indeed planet: another's song of life). Nurturing relationships based on wonder and reverence, our aim is to allow our consciousness to be utterly filled with the song of life."*

(Restall-Orr, 2008)

Chapter 9. Thinking about the community

The general community and charity.

Before we can consider our position within the Pagan community, I believe that we need to examine our attitude to the world at large in the broader community.

Giving food to a starving person is a good act regardless of what the givers spiritual beliefs are. If I were a starving person, I would be less interested in the giver's motivation or religion than the act itself. As an anonymous but sagacious person wrote: *"Your beliefs don't make you a better person; your behaviour does."* Incidentally, although many Pagans work hard and fundraise for many general secular charitable organisations (especially those concerned with wildlife and the environment), there is one specific Pagan charity called PaganAid (Chandler, I., 2016)

Whilst there are a few small Pagan charities, the general consensus has been 'why reinvent the wheel?' There are plenty of national and international charities that already protect wildlife, rain forests and vulnerable people, so why make Pagan specific versions? Occasionally there is a reason. E.g. Odinshof and the Olgar Trust bought some woodland for Pagan usage via Pagan fundraising, and some similar localised initiatives have been started. The issues begin when you consider how charities and pressure groups further their agendas: If, like Greenpeace, Extinction Rebellion and Sea Shepherd, they take direct actions instead of merely funding relief, do you always support what they do? Would you consider joining one of their protests? Not everyone can do this when they clash with work, family commitments, health and access, so some people offer to fund them instead. Do you prefer that efforts are concentrated upon negotiating with governments and big business rather than confronting them? Or do you think such actions are wasted since talking doesn't seem to have changed much? I can understand and applaud the righteous anger of the Swedish environmental activist Greta Thunberg and her ilk but feel that most movement on humanitarian or ecological issues is through a combination of approaches. I never forget the effectiveness of Bob Geldof at Live Aid, repeating on TV, *"Give them the f****** money!"* It still took practical people at charities to spend it effectively, but shamefully, politicians still haven't stopped world hunger.

Employment
Sometimes choosing a job that reflects your aims in life rather than the one that pays the most can be a distinct spiritual decision. Selecting a career in healthcare, local government, environmental agencies, social services, emergency services or education can enable one to make positive improvements not just for Pagans but the community in general. It depends upon whether one believes it is more effective working (sometimes subversively!) from the inside of institutions or being free to call them to account from outside. I went through that process myself, moving from being a sales manager to retraining as a social worker.

It can help if you privately believe you are doing work on behalf of a god or goddess sometimes. If you subscribe to the 'futility of existence' paradigm, it is doubtful whether you can fit into any religious path. You may not be able to change the world, but it is sometimes still possible to sway decision makers' opinions, even if it is an over-long process as exciting as sloth racing. One person, if vocal enough, can sometimes make a difference, primarily if a groundswell of others supports them.

If you feel that you are a lone voice in the wilderness (which is rarely true), you may not change the world. However, you can take responsibility to change your small corner of it. If you make your garden nature friendly, it may encourage neighbours to do the same. If it doesn't, at least you are doing your bit to benefit wildlife. The area that you litter pick may deter others from depositing their waste again. Your purchase of ethical products may encourage a shop to continue to stock them and be seen by other consumers. You may not be able to prevent the extinction of wildlife single-handedly, but your support of a charity (physically or financial) may stop the demise of one creature.

Dealing with other people

Does the way we interact with our deities or how we envisage them affect how we deal with other people? If we believe that we all contain the god and goddess/spirit/element within us (as opposed to them being purely external persona), then it may follow that all other people hold them as well. Or do we believe that gods and goddesses only manifest themselves within their followers? If we believe the former, then deities etc. must be found (however suppressed) within thoroughly objectionable humans. Do you believe that there are abstract forces of 'good' and 'evil' in the world, or are these just simplistic value judgements? In other words, do you believe that a person can be 'evil' or is that an over-simplification?

> *"If we remove God and his nemesis, though, the problem of evil becomes altogether human. Without a single creator and judge, there is no sin. It is our human*

fault. To the *Pagan, it is not fear of disobeying God's (or any deity's) command. That inspires his ethics; it is the fear of shame that comes when we behave in a way that is deemed dishonourable."

(Restall-Orr, E., 2007)

When meeting or dealing with other people, should we:

a. Try to find the 'good' in everyone, believing the goddess or god is in there somewhere?

b. Reject the person on the premise that they have submerged any spiritual presence by their own chosen objectionable behaviours?

c. Try to understand that the person may be influenced by a bad environment, upbringing, abuse, poverty, social status etc., so that they have an excuse for their negative behaviours?

d. Avoid interacting with them at all so as not to cause ourselves problems?

e. Challenge and confront those negative behaviours as unacceptable to you, but praise positive actions? (The Christian idea of 'hate the sin, not the sinner'   seems a parallel paradigm.)

f. Decide that the deities are external after all and not explicitly found within every human being?

By the way, there is no 'correct' answer to questions a-f. If this all seems a bit 'airy-fairy', consider this: if you were transported back to 1930s Germany and met Hitler, how would you react? Reason with him? Shoot him? Run away? If that all feels a bit remote and hypothetical, remember that there have always been evil, hate-filled tyrants and plenty continue to operate today and throughout history.

Incidentally, the British Home Office appoints paid Pagan Chaplains to visit prisons. I worked for this service for a few years in three prisons. Chaplains (the Home Office's legal term applied to all religions) can advise, educate and lead inmates in religious services within specific guidelines. Through this, H.M. Government recognises Paganism as a valid spiritual path and therefore has to respect prisoners' rights to follow it. Supposing you were asked to visit prisoners at your local prison: would you feel comfortable doing it, or do you believe they should have forfeited such rights by the nature of their crimes? They may be a murderer, rapist, paedophile, con man, gangster, drug dealer etc., who has only found out about Paganism since being sentenced. You are unlikely to know that or much about them until you meet them.

The Pagan Community
Since there has been little published research (other than numerical quantities from the Census), much of the following information has to be anecdotal, based upon my attendance of multiple Pagan camps, conferences and moots for more than 30 years, as well as frequent correspondence. However, a study of how British and American Pagans formed Pagan communities was published by Matthew Gault (2015.) He highlights the needs of many American Pagans to remain unknown by their highly Christianised societies compared to the UK, where the situation is more relaxed and debates whether making magic is an intrinsic reason for or against Pagan community cohesion. In conjunction with Lady Liberty League, the Circle Sanctuary works for Pagan rights in the USA in a similar way to the Pagan Federation in Europe & the UK. The Covenant of the Goddess (CoG) performs a similar role for Witches in the USA. In Europe, the largest Witchcraft organisation is the Children of Artemis (COA). Websites are shown at the end of this book.

The modern Pagan community comprises an enormous cross-section of society, but some characteristics are better represented than others. In the U.K., few people of ethnicities other than White British are seen at events. Whether this is through disinterest, fear of racism or other issues is not known. Unlike a century ago, few believers are of a higher social class. Few people of primary, working-class background are seen at events either, but no research has shown whether this is because of lack of finances and mobility or disinterest. Of course, there are notable exceptions to these generalisations, but we must acknowledge that our community mainly consists of middle-class white people with a good education. Being a Black Pagan can cause many problems not experienced by white Pagans, as the American 'Black Witch' indicates:

> *"Christianity is such a linchpin in the Black mindset, whatever is considered outside of the religion is considered to be an act of sheer blasphemy. Contrary to popular belief, the Black race is a very conservative race, the acceptance of something such as Paganism would come along very slowly."*

('Black Witch' 2010)

Occasionally some egotistical figure will emerge upon the national scene and make extravagant claims for their position, authority, number of followers and annoy genuine Pagans by their inevitable inaccurate and frequent interviews with the media. As they have become disparagingly known, these 'media kings or queen witches' can do a lot of short-term damage. After some inaccurate but sensational story has been published, the journalists frequently eventually discredit them, but they can cause upsets in the meantime. Fortunately, there seem to have been fewer of them appear lately, and newspapers and radio stations have begun to select better-regarded contacts. So, whilst some may say do not give them the attention they crave, what would your attitude be towards them?

It is thought that there are approximately 1 million Pagans in North America, but the US Government does not collect religious statistics. Although Adler (2006, p 20–21) stated that

American Pagans were drawn from a broad band of professions and characterised as avid readers, Magliocco researching Pagans in California, found that as in the UK

> *"The majority were "white, middle-class, well-educated urbanites."*

(Magliocco, S., 2004, p 7)

From the Pagan Federation (PF) membership statistics in the UK and Europe, gender is slightly skewed towards females, and the most popular employment sectors were social care, I.T., and artistic. The PF is an umbrella organisation for many Pagan paths within the UK and Europe. In the USA, the Covenant of the Goddess (CoG) fulfils a similar function. There also seems a tendency for Pagans to live in rural locations, but some towns and cities can muster large gatherings.

Family

You may already have a life partner or still be seeking one. Having a partner of the same spiritual path is convenient, and to some people, essential. Some couples of different faiths respect each other's views and manage to live together amicably. If it applied to you, how would you handle it? It is not just a case of each attending to their own spiritual needs, but how those needs translate into how you live. Will your partner's priorities be the same? If you have children, how will they be brought up, and which values will they be taught? That is a lot to think about when you are in love with somebody and should be discussed at an early stage to avoid heartache later.

Rites of Passage

If you are in the fortunate position of having a partner of a similar spiritual mindset, inevitably, Paganism has its rites of passage. They may be called by several names, but putting them simply:

Baby Naming: presenting the baby to the deities and naming it in front of friends and family. You may want to think about the little person at the centre of this. If you were christened into the Christian faith as a baby, without being consulted, how fair was that? As Pagans of free will, shouldn't we let the infant decide what it wants to be when they are old enough to understand? However, some see baby naming as simply asking for blessings and protection until they are older and can think for themselves.

Puberty: Not all Pagans celebrate a 'coming of age' for their children, and for most, it is an event for close family only. There are few agreed standards of when it happens for boys. Some set an age anywhere between 10 – 16, whilst others go with bodily hair appearance, voice breaking etc. Some fathers take their sons away on a weekend camp or present them with their first knife.

It is often at the time of their first menstrual cycle for girls. Frequently, this is an all-female affair, emphasising celebrating that she is a woman, with the potential to bring new life, rather than the shameful attributes prevalent in many other religions.

Handfasting: Couples (including those of the same gender) can become handfasted to show their commitment to each other. They may use this alone to seal their love, or in countries where it is not legally acknowledged, also go through a civic marriage ceremony as well. There are varying durations committed to in the non-legal handfasting by the couple. It could be *'for a year and a day'* and be renewed on an annual basis. Alternatively, it could be *'for life'*, *'so long as love shall last'* or *'eternity.'* The promises made at a handfasting vary with each couple and are frequently written individually by them. They may set the tone for the whole relationship from then. What would you want your vows to include, and for how long?

Funeral: Death is just a part of the natural cycle of life, as with the other stages. Arranging an appropriate Pagan funeral may be more complex because it may include family members who are not Pagan. It can be presided over by another local Pagan or a celebrant via the UK's LifeRites organisation. There is no required form so that you can decide upon your own form of ceremony. I have written my funeral in advance to let others know what I want, which music to use etc. It was a very liberating experience which I can recommend. It does not make death come any quicker, and I consider it the same sort of process as writing a will or taking out an insurance policy. How would you feel about doing that?

A missing stage?

To me, there appears to be a missing stage in this linear progression of life: Pagans and especially Wiccans frequently talk of the 'Maiden-Mother-Crone' progression for women. We have the first two stages represented here, but what about the third, when a woman goes through menopause and becomes the Crone? Surely that is worthy of just as much celebration and honour as the previous roles and shows respect for an Elder? Some groups may have a rite for this, and the Pluralism Project at Harvard University (USA) states that feminist Pagans have a 'croning' rite.[33]

However, I suspect that it is not widespread. Should it be? Following on from that, should there be a parallel point for men when they pass from being a father to a grandfather or Elder? It seems that I am not alone in thinking about this subject: Witch Rachel Patterson says

> *"The triple goddess is a familiar term within the pagan world (albeit not strictly an ancient one). She is usually three facets of a single Goddess or a triad of Goddesses and represents the moon phases – waxing, full and waning. Those being maiden, mother and crone. I want to add a category to this…and make it four stages – maiden, mother, matriarch, crone. I think as we now have much longer life spans and the way that we live is very different from that of our*

ancestors, we need that extra stage otherwise the jump from mother to pensioner seems too long."

(Patterson, R., 2018)

Equally, well-known witch Anna Franklin disagrees that the moon phases are similar to the triple goddess forms but says

"We have outgrown our tenure as Maidens and as Mothers, yet old age no longer follows immediately after menopause, which is why so many midlife women don't see ourselves (yet) as Crones. Where is the authentic archetype for us?"

(Franklin, A., 2017)

Intrafaith & Interfaith

There has been some positive co-operation and joint working between many UK Pagan organisations and individuals via the Heathen Pagan Symposium in recent years. In addition, several organisations in the UK facilitate networking and other services between followers of specific paths: websites for some of these appear to the book's rear. This process is known as 'Intrafaith.'

"The heart of interfaith is recognizing the common humanity of a believer you may have profound disagreements with. To find areas of commonality, to learn how to move past entrenched hostilities and prejudices. To build a world that is less violent, spiritually, emotionally, and physically."

(Pitzl-Waters, J. 2013)

Slightly more controversial is the idea of 'Interfaith,' i.e. different faiths talking to each other. Some Pagans are suspicious of this process and mistrust it, believing that other religions are using it purely to 'convert us.' That does not seem to have been the experience of those who have carried out this work, including myself. Initially, there was some resistance to Pagans becoming involved, but now that we have been, progress has been positive, if slow. It is hard to dislike or distrust someone with whom you have spent time comparing grandchildren photo's and drinking tea. It is a chance to dispel fears about the other. The role of Pagan Interfaith varies around Europe, and I am told that it is not so well developed in the USA. Mike Stygal is an ex-President of the Pagan Federation and has continued to work hard to build bridges with UK faith communities:

> *"Paganism and interfaith in Europe is at least as complex a subject as Paganism and interfaith in the UK. Different European nations have a different perspective on faith, one to another. In some nations, religion is considered extremely important, and often that translates into… one religion is extremely important, while other beliefs are viewed with varying degrees of suspicion.*
>
> *In some European nations, religion is considered important, and the diversity of religions found in those nations is embraced as a good thing. In other nations religion seems to be considered as little more than the ancient Romans considered the pagani, country dwellers. So the inclusion of Paganism in interfaith within those varied European nations is a mixed bag, and generally one that sees Paganism failing to be included in any significant way and frequently suffering discrimination."*

(Stygal, M. 2014)

I have participated in Interfaith activities, but my one criticism of the process is this: Multifaith organisations tend to attract the more liberal, educated members of each religion. Whilst they may learn much about other religions, they are not necessarily taken notice of when they return to their faith communities where others are of a more fundamentalist mindset. Sadly, I include some Pagans in that. Still, as

Churchill said, *"Meeting jaw to jaw is better than war."*[34] Many positive results have been produced from the process: joint publications, peace gardens, lectures, legislation, Civic multifaith services and practical aid to each other. Of course, any genuine conversation you choose to have with a member of another religion is technically 'Interfaith.' You have to consider whether you want to have those conversations or not and whether you support those who do?

Many Pagans blend in with their mainstream work colleagues or local community and may deliberately avoid identification by non-Pagans. This avoidance may be because they fear ridicule or persecution, but it can easily be through religion being an almost taboo subject within general English conversation. (The other taboo topics of sex, health and death maintain their hold in 'polite society' but seem to be more easily discussed now than 50 years ago.) Other Pagans will deliberately wear a jewellery item that signifies their faith, such as a ring or pendant with a pentagram, Thorshammer or Awen symbol. It is generally accepted that you are willing to answer questions about it if you openly wear such a sign. Are you ready to do that?

Local groups
If you are a sociable sort of person and want to meet and learn from others, you may consider joining a local group of some description. If you are a member of a national organisation such as a Druid order, they may be able to put you in touch with like-minded people in your area. If you are trying to join specific witch groups, such as a Gardnerian or Alexandrian coven, you will likely meet challenges. Some are well established and closed to new members, whilst others continuously have too many people on the waiting list. They will also tend to be relatively secretive and hard to find, partly to deter sensation seekers and those searching for what they perceive as 'kinky sex.' It has been difficult for some Wiccan covens to shake off the images associated with them by lurid tabloid newspaper and films of fifty years ago. Whilst sex is an

inherent part of their iconography and practice, they do not wish it to be the focal point. The issue was looked at in some detail by Jo Pearson:

> *"Wicca regards itself as disruptive. It disrupts traditional notions of religion by its inclusion of magic, at least as far as Protestantism is concerned. It disrupts accepted religious leadership by its use of the terms 'priestess' and 'high priestess' which position women powerfully. But most of all it continues to embrace the imagery of witches and witchcraft which challenge accepted social and religious norms. This is particularly so in its use of ritual nudity, sex magic (invocation, great rite, raising energy), and S/M techniques such as scourging and binding. However, for all this vaunted disruption, S/M concepts in particular have been largely abstracted into symbolic forms which strongly deny the 'inappropriate' sexuality embedded in Wiccan initiation rituals (specifically) and formative ideologies (generally) . Thus, whilst a rhetoric of disruptive sexuality is retained in Wicca, the emphasis lies in its symbolic value and 'dangerous sex' is largely forbidden. Thus, despite its often fervent claims to radicalism, openness and maturity, Wicca attempts to invoke an aura of danger and perversity whilst still embracing accepted norms of appropriate sexual behaviour, articulating a rather complex attitude towards sexuality. The resulting tension is, I would argue, a direct result of the contested spaces between theology and sexuality."*

(Jo Pearson, 2005[35])

It cannot be denied that isolated individuals may set up groups for sexual reasons, but they are very untypical and likely to be quickly denounced by other Pagans. However, sex is as much a part of nature as birth and death. To avoid sensationalism by the press, some statements issued by Pagans, particularly witches, have skirted around the issue simply to avoid being labelled perverts.

> *"Magic and sexuality have a long and complex relationship in the history of Western esotericism. Sexual magic as a sophisticated ritual technique is largely a development of the modern era, beginning in roughly the mid-nineteenth century. However, sexual magic has roots that run much deeper in Western occult and esoteric traditions, some of them historical and some of them imaginary or fantastic (Urban 2005, 21–54; Versluis 2008; Hanegraaff and Kripal 2008).*
>
> (Urban, H., 2006)

Some witches rituals have replaced sexual practices such as 'the Great Rite' (consensual sex between an adult priest and priestess within a ritual to raise power) with more symbolic actions such as plunging an athame knife into a chalice, which is probably a lot less fun! If abuse of any kind occurs, it should be reported to the police to deal with, just like any other situation. It is not our role to be investigators, prosecutors and judges, and the most Pagan organisations can do is cancel membership.

If you attend a Pagan moot (regular general meetings of Pagan discussion groups, mainly in pubs or cafes), you may be able to make contact with ritual groups after having established yourself as a regular member. Specialist magazines and the internet are also sources of contacts but beware of people showing an over-keenness for you to join them. Are they who they say they are? Do their interests ethics match yours? Are they out to gain power, money or sexual favours? There are the occasional bad apples, so beware and treat contacts the same as if you were going on a blind date. Try and find out as much as possible about the path they take, how many members, whether there is an initiation or even ritual nudity (skyclad), an accepted practice in a few covens.

Do not be too offended if you are rejected for membership in a group. As Gault says;

> *"community construction is a dynamic process which requires a magical group to balance individual egos and beliefs with communally agreed beliefs and restrictions."*

(Gault, M. 2015, p.23)

You may be regarded as a perfectly good person by them but unsuitable for the group dynamic. They may be nervous about disrupting a group dynamic that has taken time and trouble for them to achieve and not want to upset that balance. They may simply wish to keep a balance between male and female members.

It is helpful to know in advance that the average Pagan group may have a short life before dissolving. I understand the average life of a core group is about three years, but there are exceptions: some have functioned for decades now whilst others fizzle out after a few months. Sometimes a few of the members then form another one. Can you face this frustration, or would you prefer to go solo rather than start all over again?

A two and half year study beginning in 1992 was published by Amy Simes of group transformation amongst East Midlands Pagans.[36] The situation was very fluid due to rapid growth in the number of visible Pagans and groups set up to accommodate them at that time. However, she did identify that some people were 'serial joiners' of groups whilst others were solitary for a while, dipped their toe into a group and then returned to solitary practice. Enthusiastic group members may attend more than one activity, e.g. a pub moot, a pathworking group and a working ritual group. They may also be involved in drumming groups, historical re-enactment and morris dancing that are not strictly esoteric organisations but which attract many Pagans.

Pagan camps and conference events.

You are welcome to wear whatever you like at most Pagan events. Some wear special robes and cloaks for rituals, but those who don't are not thought out of place. Visually, many modern Pagans present flamboyant fashions at their events. Gothic black seems to have been superseded by hippyish multi-coloured outfits by both genders or steampunk attire. Even those who sport more mainstream clothes tend to join the trend of wearing an excess of mainly silver jewellery, including symbolic pendants, bangles and rings for both sexes.

Laughter, enjoyment of folk and rock music, alcohol, easily shared conversation and hugs are commonplace. There will often be stalls supplying esoteric crafts, jewellery, clothing, books and art. Are such craftspeople and the musicians entitled to earn a living wage? *"I could make it cheaper than what they are charging"* is a comment I have overheard more than once. My questions back to them are, *"Why don't you make it for yourself then? Will you declare tax on your earnings? Will you have petrol expenses, an awning to buy and a site fee to pay? Will the price you charge cover that, plus a minimum living wage per hour for the work making it and selling it?"*

Similarly, some people expect musicians to appear for free; do they expect them to get their instruments, p.a., van and rehearsal room for free? Loving to play doesn't really cover that! Likewise, would you wish to get the companies providing the portaloos, marquees, walkie talkies and safety lighting to do so for free on the basis that you do not want to pay them? They are all providing a service, after all.

Enjoying yourself and networking with other like-minded people seems to be the principal aims of most people attending UK Pagan camps in my experience. Attending concerts, rituals, and lectures has a lower priority for some people, and some may not participate in any of those latter activities, instead enjoying eating, drinking, and chatting. There may be the occasional drunk person, but these are usually dealt with sympathetically by the organisers. Open use of illegal drugs is generally forbidden but may carry on within the privacy of tents. The situation seems to have been different elsewhere. In the USA, the Reclaiming camps are expressly no-alcohol, no-drug. One of the best known Pagan activists in the USA, Starhawk, the influential author of *The Spiral Dance* (1979), who runs them, explained:

> *"For us, this policy came out of a time in our community when a lot of people were in Alcoholics Anonymous or other 12-step programmes around addictions of one sort or another. But we also found that it created an atmosphere for our public rituals that we liked. It kind of separated out the people who were coming for some kind of serious ritual work, from the people who might just be coming to party."*

(Starhawk 2001 p.13)

At least one UK Pagan camp set up principally for learning has changed its ethos in recent years because of a mismatch between casual attendees and serious students. Still, most events run serious activities mainly during the day and more relaxed entertainment in the evening. You may need to research events and then decide which sort you want to attend. Whether a particular conference or camp is suitable for children and non-Pagans is another consideration.

For a culture notably free in their attitudes towards sexual matters, most people arrive with a partner and stay with them, and attitudes towards the LGBT+ community are generally positive. Hale (2012) reports that some Pagan festivals in the USA may be freer in their attitudes towards sexual partners being acquired over their duration.

Joint rituals

Some events may have a timetable of speakers, workshop sessions and other activities whilst others are less formalised. The majority will have a group ritual that everyone can take part in if they wish. Some are highly organised, with volunteers taking specific roles to lead chants, make invocations, or distribute food and drink (generically known as 'cakes and ale' but maybe bread and wine etc.)

This may all sound splendid on the face of it: Pagans from various orientations working together in mutual harmony to produce a meaningful experience for participants. That is generally the intention, but it can present you with dilemmas:

Whilst some ritual leaders will seek to become 'all-inclusive,' some may acknowledge specific gods and goddesses but leave your particular favourites out. After all, a mixture of Pagan's are interested in thousands of deities from many mythologies. So do you keep quiet, add yours in with a whisper under your breath or sulk? If you know the ritual's nature beforehand is not to your taste, should you avoid joining in with it? Some traditions name their deities 'the Lord & Lady.' Use of this nomenclature can have an advantage in diverse Pagan settings, as the internationally known witch and writer Janet Farrar explained to Gulik:

> *"When we work, when we are working as a unit, we just use the term Lord and Lady. But when we're working individually and on our own, we work with our personal deity. So that means that when we come together as a group, their Lord and Lady are totally different from my Lord and Lady."*

> *(Janet Farrar cited in Gulak, 2017 p.17)*

The same disparity applies to many familiar Pagan chants. I do not join in with the ones where I can't entirely agree with the sentiments, whilst others may join in for the sake of unity.

Being a Heathen, I am frequently at odds with many statements taken for granted by others. E.g. We regard the moon as male and the sun as female, the reverse of most other Pagan mythologies. I take a general attitude that more connects the various Pagan paths than divides us, so I try to co-operate whenever possible. How you deal with such things is down to personal choice and may be based upon firmly held beliefs that you may feel cannot be compromised. I have certainly received a lot of stick from a minority of my fellow Heathens and other Pagans by compromises I have made at times to enable some form of Pagan unity, whilst others do not have to face such dilemmas. If they are not involved in intrafaith (co-operation between Pagan paths) or even interfaith (co-operation between Pagans and other religions for some joint initiatives), they do not have to face these issues. I consciously chose to do so but can understand the reluctance of others who feel uncomfortable with those choices. This includes Heathen separatists who disagree that Heathenism can be associated with Paganism.

The problem of catering for a diverse 'congregation' is a problem that ritual organisers encounter. The danger is that if they neutralise everything that may be contentious for one person or another, the whole ritual can be inoffensive but terribly bland. Some take the view that it is better to have an annual ceremony in a different style each time: Celtic Witchcraft this year, Druid the next, Heathen the one after etc.

Ritual and event organisers should consider alternatives for Pagans of different abilities as well: I can no longer stand still for more than about ten minutes, so I need the option of sitting on a chair or perching or my shooting stick. Others with wheelchairs and mobility scooters may not be able to deal with rough terrain. Does this mean that the event should shift indoors if there is no hard and even surface?

What adjustments should be made for Pagans for whom English is not their principal language if it is an international event? I have already spotted sign language interpreters at some events for the deaf. However, when the event is small and put on at low cost by people in their own time, how far should we expect them to go? You may be in a similar position one day, so you need to sort out your preferences, which will, in turn, be based upon your ethics and the way that you intend to relate to the whole Pagan community.

Although many Pagans arrange their own handfast weddings, baby namings and funerals themselves, there is a national organisation set up called LifeRites that will assist with obtaining a celebrant in your area and provide some training for them. Their website is at the rear of this book.

Shops and consumerism

The role of specialist esoteric shops (and stalls at events) within the Pagan community is essential. They frequently become the meeting place for like minds, the place to find 'interesting' posters, acquire incense, oils, ritual objects, tarot cards, magazines and books. Most work on the goodwill of their owners, and some provide training courses and divination. Inevitably to keep afloat in a small niche market, they also have to appeal to a non-Pagan public sector. They may not enjoy stocking rainbow coloured unicorns, angel cards, and crystals mined with explosives, but New Agers and the general public help keep them in business.

> *"For many Pagans the New Age is stripped of tradition, and has no roots, either in history or in a particular cultural background. Therefore, the whole New Age movement can be seen by Pagans as – metaphorically and literally   speaking – "weekend spirituality", as it may not have a major influence on the social behaviour, ethics or political opinions of its followers."*

(Anczyk, A. & Vencálek, M. 2013 p.162)

Shopkeepers may even have to put up with verbal and physical attacks from fundamentalist religious opponents as one of our community's visible signs. They need all the support they can get! Supporting your local businesses is always a good thing (rather than big company mail order) but supporting esoteric shops is a worthwhile activity. There is, however, sometimes a tension between wanting lots of 'prettys' and the frequent Pagan ethos of anti-consumerist, anti-capitalist ideas:

> *"I don't buy "pagan stuff." No crystals (mined destructively from the Earth), no chalices or blades or wands or new Tarot decks. Sometimes I'm tempted, but I don't do it. Well, other than candles. I already have enough incense to last the rest of my life, stored carefully so as to remain fresh and pungent. I don't take great pride in this, because the fact is that 25-30 years ago, I DID accumulate some of that stuff. I have enough "things" to dress a Focus (altar) and to symbolize all the various qualities and attributes I might wish to include in a ritual. I'm a bit short on ritual clothing, but it's quite rare that I might need it, and I make do (I have plenty of other costuming, some of which can be adapted in a pinch). But mostly, now, I simply work with what I have. Or I make stuff from found materials.*

> *And I'm a little torn about this, because I have friends who make their livings selling "pagan stuff": masks and headdresses and ritual tools and costuming…yes, and candles and incense and statuettes and all that witchy occult stuff that the ritualist may desire. But I have become a radically minimalist consumer. I have more than enough "stuff", and feeding the machine that grinds the Sacred natural world into money is not consistent with my values. The machine named capitalism."*

The Pagan Thinker

(Green, M. 2018)

If you do seek 'Pagan stuff' and haven't got an esoteric shop in your area, there are many small online Pagan suppliers. However, if it is English language specialist books that you are after, there are three major Esoteric bookshops in London of some years standing reputations, and each has mail order facilities: Atlantis, Treadwells & Watkins bookshops all have their websites listed at the rear of this book.

As a Pagan, you may have to review your whole role as a consumer: do you insist on ethically sourced meat or become a vegetarian? How about organically grown vegetables – shouldn't you be avoiding farming methods that poison the land with chemicals? How about your cleaning materials, clothes, energy providers? Should you be seeking the most ethical solution rather than the cheapest? Are you insisting on minimal packaging to avoid waste? Are you seeking second hand, recycled goods instead of buying new ones whenever you can? Although buying secondhand or growing your vegetables saves money, some options tend to have a higher price. With a limited budget, what compromises can you make and which expenditure has priority? How far will you go, and do you need to make sacrifices in some areas to pay for all of this? From Paganism starting as a casual interest, issues like this affect daily living and may bring you into conflict with your household members less committed to your ideals. Being an Eco-Warrior is so much more than chaining yourself to a tree.

Disputes

Unsurprisingly, for a group of passionately involved in a religion with no orthodoxy, occasional disputes occur. Sometimes they are merely local divisions over an organisation or personal dynamics rather than religious schisms. Sometimes disputes can be far broader and even international. Arguments about the authenticity of various witchcraft initiatory histories have been one subject in dispute. A much larger global discussion centred around whether there was a continuing tradition linking witches back to ancient times and whether Gerald Gardner carried on a tradition that he found or simply invented his own.

Notably, academic opinions from Dr Aiden Kelly (1991) in the USA and Prof. Ronald Hutton in the U.K. were the cause of much heated debate. (Hutton, 2003 p. 265-7) Hutton faced the wrath of many Pagans when he also challenged the historical construction of the eight-fold ritual year:

> *"It was only in the late nineteenth century that British scholars in general concluded that the megalithic monuments belong to the New Stone Age and the Druids to the Iron Age, almost three thousand years later, severing the link. This news took another hundred years to reach the general public. It was likewise only in the early twentieth century that Welsh academics proved conclusively that Iolo had made up his Druidic system. They did so, moreover, in books published in Welsh, so that there are members of the English and American public, to this day, who still believe in it. Among those who long retained such a belief were various orders of modern Druids inspired, at least in part, by Iolo's dream; and some of these celebrated rites inside Stonehenge at midsummer from 1912 onward (Hutton 2007, 64 – 75 and 174– 93). In this manner, one-half of the modern Pagan cycle was put into place."*

(Hutton, R., 2008 p.254)

N.B. 'Iolo' = late 18th century Druid pioneer Iolo Morganwg aka Edward Williams

I believe Hutton (1996) has done more for Paganism, Druidry, Asatru and Witchcraft's proper research than anyone else alive, both by his own efforts and inspiring and ground-breaking for others.

The internet community

Pagans were some of the internet's early users, and a good proportion of them either work with Information Technology or are pretty tech-savvy. I remember when the Pagan Federation switched from physical national committee meetings to sometimes using the internet. Not only did it save members travelling for large distances across the UK and beyond to attend (saving time and travel expenses), we were able to make quicker decisions and get more done.

I believe it also appeals to the creative side exhibited by many Pagans. Individuals and organisations have produced some imaginative and artistic websites to inform others of their aims and ideas.

For some Pagans, the internet constitutes their only communication with other Pagans. It may consist of passively reading the contents of the many Pagan websites that exist, or they may interact utilizing chat groups on social media such as Facebook or web forums. As many Pagans live isolated from others (being in the minority of most population groups), this is an excellent practical method to exchange ideas, ask questions and gain support in what may otherwise seem a lonely path to tread. (To paraphrase a popular TV programme, 'The only Pagan in the village.') However, it is not without pitfalls: if it becomes the only action you take as a Pagan, are you living a Pagan life anymore or becoming an armchair spectator? Sometimes, furious, passionate debates scare off gentler souls who want their spiritual lives to be peaceful. Occasionally internet trolls cause mayhem until moderators of forums remove them. Yet, the internet forms an integral part of the Pagan community, including many very active Pagans. Commenting on the alt.pagan web forum, Grieve says:

> *"The users of alt.pagan utilize the 'energy' of a personal religion to imagine a virtual religious community. What binds together the myriad of 'personal religions° which make up alt.pagan is not presence. Instead, these*

individual practitioners are able to form a virtual community because of the affective sentiment which is perceived by them to be produced by the ritualized imagination. The ritualized imagination — the sanctification not of the content of specific creative acts, but of the act of creation itself — phenomenologically produces 'energy."

(Grieve, G. 1995 p.111)

That 'energy' may occasionally be explicitly raised by an internet group in an online ritual in place of a physical ceremony, demonstrating the creative use of technology not usually found in other religions' online presence.

How far will you become involved in online Paganism? It is sometimes difficult to avoid if wanting to attend a Pagan camp or conference. Booking and details are only likely to be made available in this way, being both a cheap and eco-friendly method compared to conventional written mail. Yet, it is very easy to become 'sucked into' a time-consuming daily routine of interacting with numerous internet forums and chat groups, as I know to my cost! How will you manage to strike a balance?

Chapter 10. Thinking about Magic

The Cambridge Dictionary defines the word 'miracle' to be:

> *"an unusual and mysterious event that is thought to have been caused by a god because it does not follow the usual laws of nature."*

Yet change the word for 'miracle' to 'magic', and the definition is:

> *"the use of special powers to make things happen that would usually be impossible, such as in stories for children."*

There seems to be some religious bias there for what should be an unbiased academic source. If Jesus does a miracle like turning water into wine, it is caused by a god. If a Pagan tried to do the same ('by use of special powers'), that would be impossible and only fit for children's stories." So either the water can get changed into wine or not, depending on which stories you believed when told as a child about the wedding in Cana in the Gospel of St. John from the Bible. Indeed 'magic' is an alternative way of saying 'miracle' and vice versa. Whether you choose to believe in it is up to you. After all, Arthur C. Clarke said that *"Any sufficiently advanced technology is indistinguishable from magic."*[37]

It is sometimes difficult to identify whether a Pagan ceremony is purely to acknowledge gods, ancestors, and other supernatural beings, get in touch with nature, or do some magic. The challenge is to separate these three elements: since getting in touch with such beings could be interpreted as magical in itself, how is that separated from healing or bringing good luck? Ian Corringham gives us food for thought in this comparison with what happens in other religious paths:

> *"The only useful definition of magic as separate from religion that I've been able to come up with lately is the application of spiritual power for personal world goals. Basically, there's almost no difference in form between magic and religion. If you're a Catholic you're using bread for the host, reciting Hail Marys and making prayers to the Trinity in order to do your spells, and if you're a Hindu you're making sacrifices and doing austerities and drawing yantras, etc. In Hinduism, occultism is entirely integrated, it's present throughout. The real practice of ritual at big temples required all sorts of occult doo-dah on the part of their priesthood, it's very integrated. Then you get to something like Zen Buddhism and it's all about sitting quietly and waiting to be enlightened. In Japan it's all mixed up with Shinto sorcery, and all that stuff left over from Taoism."*

(Corrigan, I., (2019)

Few Pagans do specific spells; many don't even believe in magic other than the wonder of nature, seasons, new life etc. Yet most spiritual paths contain an element of magic within the beliefs: it may be labelled differently (particularly in other religious paths) as 'miracles' or 'god-like activities.'

Sometimes, the most significant act of magic we can perform is to continue living happily or transform our lives by learning lessons and applying them. Very few people know themselves. If we can work towards that, many other questions are answered: our attitude towards the world is likely to change. An old friend of mine from the West Country said

> *"In witchcraft, doing things, taking action and making things are as important as words. Rituals are a vital part of serving the gods, but practical and often simple, direct actions are an essential part of magic-making. Magic is something that should be lived. Much of the magic in this book is about apparently simple things, such as sitting out in a forest all day, standing in the moonlight, collecting berries or pebbles, or looking at the sea in a mirror. It is my belief that these things, experienced with all the senses, and done with intent, can be deep forms of magic and have the most profound effect, and be just as powerful as complex rituals, if not more so."*

(Morgan, L. 2013 p.8)

Specific use of magic

The majority of books about doing magic tend to be based on witchcraft, ancient and modern. However, be aware that this is not the only choice: there are books about the magic and runes of the Heathen (aka Asatru, Northern, Odinist) tradition and information on ancient Egyptian, Greek and Roman practices. In addition, there is information and even experiential courses on Shamanic journeying. If you want to get a good understanding of Shamanism before getting into it, why not read *'The Way of the Shaman'* (Harner, 1982)? You may also find some forms of magic in traditions that run alongside Paganism but are not always part of it. E.g. Chaos magic, Angelic Magic[38], Quabbalistic, Traditional (pre-Gardnerian)[39] etc. They are often quite complex in their structure and relationships with religions and need independent research away from 'mainstream' Pagan literature.

Some may query, "where does the magic come from?" It is a fair enough question, but you will have to find your answer. I will, however, introduce you to a writer that has had more influence on me outside of Heathenism than any other, the late American Druid Isaac Bonewits discussing men personifying objects and ideas:

> *"The universal tendency to make our gods and demons in our own image: not to mention the theological point that manlike gods justify childish behaviour on the part of people. So our key phrase for this law will be: Anything can be a person.*
>
> *The Laws of Invocation and Evocation say that you can conjure up from, respectively, the inside of and outside of your metapattern, real entities."*

(Bonewits, 1989 p.16)

Inevitably, if you mix within the Pagan world or read the books, you have to work out for yourself whether it is genuine and do you want to do it? This is not a book for discussing spells, magical techniques and 'how to do it.' This is the book to ask you what your attitude to it is? If you choose not to believe in it, that is your choice, but as Roald Dahl said, *"Those who don't believe in magic will never find it."* The well-known shaman Leo Rutherford of Eagle Wing, UK, said

> *"The commonplace statement 'Oh it's only imagination' is a gross denial of not only the whole realm of the magical but of the any understanding of how the universe really works. It is in the imagination, the thought or dream realm where all is conceived and of*

which this familiar third dimension of gross material reality, the 'tonal', is but a reflection, and it is there in the realm of cause that the shaman works. For example – consider the room or building you are sitting in, or a building nearby. What came first, 'reality' or the thought? Surely the thought…"

(Rutherford, L., 2011)

Many believe that one must possess a strong personality, well-developed ego and confidence to know your specific will and project it to succeed at magic. I agree with them. It could be the reason why so many of our early Pagan pioneers and ritual magicians fell out so spectacularly and frequently. I suspect a clash of egos was sometimes more responsible for such acrimonious disputes rather than any divergence of opinions.

I have to be open and say that I believe in magic and sometimes try to use it. It does not have guaranteed results and is an art rather than a science. It isn't easy to prove the veracity of, since the resultant actions may have happened anyway. I always believe in doing the practical, straightforward things first to produce the desired result, or it could even be a coincidence. If it is a medical problem, see a doctor. If it is a legal matter, see a solicitor. If it is a personal problem, dare to speak out about it. Having done that, I see no harm in enhancing the process with some magic to help it go smoother. In this way, magic becomes a 'complementary practice' to health, law or psychology, instead of being an 'alternative practice' that negates other scientifically based solutions. Pagans, in general, are not anti-science, and many are scientifically qualified.

"Pagans are non-dogmatic and empirical; they are more concerned with whether a ritual or spell works than how it works (Starhawk, 1999: 220; interviewees A, C and F), and they tend to be ambivalent about the practice of magic, justifying it sometimes as a

The Pagan Thinker

psychologically beneficial but metaphorical practice, and sometimes as possibly being effective in the sense of getting results (Luhrmann, 1989: 335)."

(Aburrow, Y., 2008 p.61)

Aburrow also concludes that some Pagans sometimes see science and mythology as explaining things from different viewpoints, both of which are valid. *"Most do not view science and religion as being in conflict, but as complementary modes of viewing the world (Luhrmann's 'metaphorical' position)."* (Aburrow, Y., 2008 p.61)

Ethical questions

However, as soon as we get into using magic (whether successful or not), we venture into ethical dilemmas, maybe where the idea of 'black magic' and 'white magic' enter. I believe that most magic, by its very nature, tends to be a muddy grey mixture.

Let me explain: most pain is a body's reaction to warn that something is wrong and often utilised to immobilise or take better care of that limb or organ. Therefore, if we use magic to heal, we must understand that it may have consequences. That patient may try to do more than they should when the pain is relieved, causing further injury or illness. So was that magic black, white or grey? If they are informed of the possible outcome, e.g. the leg will be less painful, but heavy exercise will worsen it, then the responsibility lies with the recipient not to abuse the pain relief. That is why making healing magic for someone who does not know about it and has not given permission is a violation of their right to choose. They may rather suffer than accept pain relief other than via their religion or a doctor.

Robert Cochrane (aka Roy Bowers), the founder of the Clan of Tubal Cain, said[40]:

"Nothing is purely good or evil, these are relative terms that man has hung upon unacceptable mysteries. To my particular belief the Goddess, white with works of good, is also black with works of darkness, yet both of them are compassionate, albeit the compassion is a cover for the ruthlesness of total Truth."

Another popular reason for people to attempt magic (both in the past and present) is commonly known as love magic. It tries to get two people romantically together, generally at the request of one of them and with the other's ignorance. Hence if it is successful, the target of affection has their right to choose a partner freely, subverted. Once again, we face the shadowy area that can be worsened if one of the partners is secretly unsavoury: a gold digger, philanderer, or abuser. Suddenly what was intended as a 'good' piece of magic is turned 'bad' by the consequences. There are many more examples like these: environmental protests that prevent people from gaining employment and homes or diverts a road to a more environmentally fragile place than initially planned.

If we believe in the power of magic, should we use it? It can be a deceptive mistress that is too appealing to ignore. Should we seek permission? Should we interfere? Is it unethical to wish harm on another person, even if they have done wrong?.

"Contemporary Western paganism has attempted to harness this violation with ethics. It speaks in terms of the law of threefold return. What the magician or pagan practitioner does, that is, sends out, returns three times, or three times as strong. This law of threefold return is claimed to apply to good and bad actions alike."

(York, 2003 p. 69)

One has to question whether this 'law of threefold return' has an ancient pedigree or a modern invention to salve consciences? What about cursing? If you can send positive magic, you are also capable of sending harmful spells. Surely that must be an ethical no-no? What about the earlier example of meeting Hitler? Wouldn't it have been justified to have cursed him so that he failed to gain power and carry out his terrible plans? Some English witches are believed to have done so.[41] You certainly would not have attained his permission! Don't forget that a group of Nazi occultists worked on his side and sent known magicians to concentration camps who did not support them: not everything in the occult world is sweetness and light. He may be gone, but many modern evil politicians may still seem a legitimate target.

High Magic

The examples above refer to what is sometimes termed 'Low Magic' or 'Natural Magic.' Magic is sometimes divided into the "High" magic of the intellectual elite, using complex procedures and tools bordering on science. The "Low" magic of common folk practices used by witches, cunning men etc. If the ethical arguments in the preceding section have put you off from going anywhere near magic, then let me make a distinction.

There is inevitably a separate concept of 'High Magic.' The term 'High Magic' is a contested one. Some believe that it is all magic that promotes the spiritual progression of the individual performing it, or in other words, 'working on oneself.' This is solely concerned with developing you as an individual: exploring your own identity and mind, getting rid of negative influences, and becoming in tune with the infinite powers. It is hard to think of this as unethical since you take responsibility for it, and theoretically, it does not directly affect anyone else. Now comes the big but! Such work is inevitably intense and will require your utmost powers of concentration and effort. It is unlikely that you will have any mentor to guide you. It will inevitably cause mental strain as you disassemble yourself in rituals more destructive than you would ever experience in psychoanalysis. If you have responsibilities towards a partner, family, career, it is likely to affect them adversely. Unless you are a 'free agent', can you accept that responsibility and possibility? Some processes may take extended continuing periods of time. As Manon Hedenborg-White says:

> "Some Pagans view gods and goddesses in psychological terms, as archetypes of the human mind. Magic and ritual are not distinguishable from religion in Pagan practice but are viewed as means to spiritual transformation."

(Hedenborg-White, M. 2014)

There is a second concept of 'High Magic' that others adhere to: it may still be used for personal gnosis (spiritual mysteries). Still, it can also be used for other purposes such as influencing exterior events and people. It almost always has Ceremonial Magic as its working method. Ceremonial Magic is complex, and much of it derives from the work of the Hermetic Order of the Golden Dawn, especially the use of Qaballah. It may also draw upon mediaeval grimoires, alchemical texts, the Enochian magic of the Elisabethan Dr Dee, Eliphas Levi, Agrippa, Hermeticism and the Thelemic work of Aleister Crowley and much more such as the work 'The Magus' by Francis Barrett (1801)

Equipment

Dependent on your path in magic, you may also require expensive robes, temple and equipment. This especially applies to what is known as 'Ceremonial Magic.' Of course, some other paths do not need any equipment or robes to do magic or celebrate festivals. Some ways do not even have a concept of 'higher magic.' New converts frequently buy or make equipment and robes. Sometimes kit such as a wand, athame, candles, etc. gives confidence to a person as props and adds to a ritual space's general ambience. Some continue to use them and add to them over time. Others tend to use them less and less and discover that a pointed finger is just as effective as a wand – it is just a matter of confidence and not having to put on a show for others or yourself. It is much easier to carry around with you as well and hard to detect by others! So how do you feel about acquiring magical paraphernalia?

Chapter 11. Thinking about the future

The well-known and respected Scottish witch John McIntyre sees a future of better-integrated Paganism in Scotland: as ex PF Scotland President, he and his wife Kitty Mcintyre and their friends had a lot to do with that. They got into the new Scottish Parliament's start-up process and established that religious equality was factored into new initiatives. Unlike the rest of the UK, one can legally be married in a Pagan handfast wedding in Scotland, thanks to their efforts. In looking to the future, one hopes the rest of Gt. Britain will revise its archaic laws to follow that lead.

> *"Paganism isn't a religion to which people are converted. It's one they find their own way into after realising it's what they've always been. Accepting that you're a Pagan brings no sense of revelation, still less of salvation, but simply a feeling of 'coming home'.*

> *While Pagans are, and probably always will be, a small minority within Scottish society, most of us do not feel at all isolated as some characteristic Pagan attitudes –*

sexual equality, environmental responsibility and religious tolerance among them – are also now shared by large sections of the wider society. The Pagan community is not insular and does not seek to hold itself apart. Nearly all of us are well integrated into the wider society.

In many ways, Pagans are well suited to this increasingly diverse Scotland because Paganism takes pride in being a very diverse religion within itself. Understandings of the Divine in modern Paganism largely arise from, and are sustained by, personal experience of the sacred within Nature rather than through the authority of the written word. It appears fairly obvious to most of us that religion is less a matter of absolute truths than of subjective understandings that may be appropriate to those who hold them but are by no means universal. When we look at Nature – as Pagans tend to do rather   frequently – we see that a great diversity of plant and animal species makes for healthier, stronger and more beautiful ecosystems. To Pagans, a great diversity of beliefs and practices makes for healthier, stronger and more   beautiful religion."

(Mcintyre, J., 2016)

'How long before we can be open about our beliefs' is a frequent question from more reserved Pagans, afraid of abuse, prejudice and worse. Sometimes those fears are worse than the reality: despite my openness, I have not encountered too many attacks, but maybe it is because of my size, confidence, appearance and general attitude. I can, however, feel sympathy for those who are not so fortunate. If those of us who can be public in our beliefs and challenge any negativity do so, it will become easier for others. We need more people like teacher Arietta Bryant, who took up her head teachers offer for non-Christians to come to school on 'Xmas Jumper

Day' in their own religion's ceremonial garments. She went in her Pagan Priestess robes and head-dress!

> *"I would like more Pagans to feel free to be open about their spirituality. I firmly believe that the more public we become and the more we are willing to answer people's questions, then the more normalised Paganism will become. Eventually, saying that you are a Pagan will no more raise an eyebrow than if you say you are a Christian."*

> (Bryant, A. 2016 p. 101-103)

Research

If some of my comments about academia in Chapter 6 seem harsh, I believe their interactions with the Pagan world are improving. Melissa Harrington is a Witch who has worked on Pagan studies within the academic world. She seems optimistic in her view of the future:

> *"I think the study of contemporary Pagan Witchcraft has only just scraped the surface of what it could be, and that academia can work in a very effective dialogue with scholars and practitioners. I hope that as Pagan studies progresses it will continue to strive for honesty and reflexivity, with all Pagans out of the broom closet, as their human right, and part of a wider ranging scholarly necessity. What I do know is that as Pagan studies grows it will continue to provide a vital view of contemporary religion, community, identity, and belief, and remain at the forefront of developing new resources for studying humanity and its dilemmas, drives and dreams in the twenty-first century; and I am be proud to be a part of this."*

> (Harrington, M., 2015)

We already see the results of better quality research from Pagans and academics as they become less suspicious of each other. If you had the opportunity, what would you want to research or have other people research on your behalf?

Globalisation

The globalisation of ideas is hard to prevent, even if someone should want to do so. Gardner and other Pagans' opinions who followed him in the UK have already spread to other places. There are Gardnerian and Alexandrian witch covens in the USA, many parts of Europe and elsewhere. Inevitably these newly seeded religious communities adapt to local conditions and create their unique communities.

Just as First Nation Americans and Australian Aborigines have rightly criticised Western civilisation for cultural misappropriation of their ideas, how long will it be before British style Paganism is no longer seen as a purely UK phenomenon? In some cases, it was introduced (sometimes by British ex-pats) into places that already had their own native traditions. E.g. Hexencrafte in the Pennsylvania Dutch country, Strega in Italy. Heathenism was revived in England, Iceland, and Australia and re-introduced into Scandinavia and Germany. While some Pagan musicians and lecturers such as myself are invited to other countries, the internet enables an unlimited amount of international cross-fertilisation of ideas at a general level.

Legacy

Carolyn Hillyer and her partner Nigel Shaw are well known in the UK Pagan community as musicians, but they took on a small farm in the wilds of Dartmoor and created a shrine for ceremonies on their land. In an interview with Manda Scott, she reflected upon passing on a legacy:

> *"And so it's up to us to be able to bear witness and we who've been working this journey for a long time and moving into a different part of our lives that we are bearing witness and holding energy for this younger collective voice to represent humanity. And we mustn't*

hold on to things ourselves because it's dependent on us to keep allowing the flow, keep allowing it to move through our fingers."

(Manda Scott, 2021)

That desire to pass on some of what we have learnt or achieved to our next generation has not gained much momentum yet. Maybe it is due to Pagans not involving under-18-year-olds in the past when they could. Nowadays, many more events are family-friendly whilst still acknowledging the need not to indoctrinate young minds and let them make their own spiritual quests when they are ready.

Some of the more youthful are creating new forms of Paganism in ignorance or opposition to an old fogey like me. Good for them! They should reflect our original anarchic roots and challenge everything lest our generation becomes the new orthodoxy. They will be more likely to form a group on social media than by meeting people at a moot. However, it would be unfortunate if the Pagan babies were thrown out with the sacred bathwater.

In the last 100 or so years, we have lost numerous pioneers, researchers, activists, leaders and writers of modern European and American Paganism and Witchcraft. In no particular order: Gerald Gardner, Dorien Valiente, Alex Sanders, Osman Spare, Florence Farr, Kenneth Grant, Rosaleen Norton, Cunning James Murrell, Andrew Chumbley, Oberon Zell, Fred Lamond, Jean Williams, Zach Cox, Sarah Kay, Alex Sanders, Robert Cochrane, Evan John Jones, Alastair Clay-Egerton, Ross Nichols, Raymond Buckland, AE Waite, Michael Howard, Sir Charles Frazer, Ralph Harvey, Dion Fortune, Annie Besant, Robert Graves, Marija Gimbutas, Bernard King, Gwen Thompson, Olivia Robertson, Amanda Class-Hamilton, Cecil Williamson, Victor Anderson, Timothy Leary, Gavin Frost, Charles Leland, John Belham-Payne, HR Giger, Sybil Leek, Ken Rees, Diane Firmin, John Score, Macgregor Mathers, Eliphas Levi, Guido von List, Pamela

The Pagan Thinker

Colman-Scott, Carlos Castaneda, Stewart Farrar, Robert Graves, Gerald Suster, Aleister Crowley, Carl Weschke, George Pickingill, Margot Adler, Jack Gale, Helena Blavatsky, Steve Wilson, Madeline Montalban, WB Yeats, Israel Regardie, Isaac Bonewits and all of the original members of the Golden Dawn and Theosophist organisations.

Doubtless, I have missed out on some worthy names that I have forgotten or of which I was not aware. No discourtesy or insult is intended. Similarly, within the next 50 years, we will likely lose many more prominent community members, many of whom, like me, are now of at least retirement age. The above list is not an 'In Memorium' feature: it is a wake-up call to say that we owe it to our future generations to inform them of our history as the first generations of modern Paganism. Just as Christians, Moslems, Hindus, etc., value their early holy men and women's memories and teachings, so should we. As what has been classed by some as a 'new religious movement' (NRM), we should give future generations clues about how our movement started, the struggles, and how it developed. Already the details and stories of these people are frequently being lost, mythologised or forgotten. Sable Aradia delivered a presentation at the Canadian National Pagan Conference where she asked the audience to think about 'Reawakening a Pagan Theology.'

> *"Everything we write, everything we blog, everything we say about the subject, will become foundational doctrine for the Pagans of the future. That is, if Pagans exist in the future; and that's by no means assured, especially if we're willing to bury what makes us unique in the mire of fads and popular opinion. Think of it! Someday someone in a school of theology, pursuing the future equivalent of a doctorate of divinity, will quote the works of Brendan Myers or Kerr Cuhulain in the same essay as the writings of St. Augustine!"*
>
> (Aradia, S., 2013)

The Pagan Thinker

How we inform the future is open to question. Firstly, many of the books from our era are unlikely to survive. Those that do may not be what we would perceive as accurate or representative. It is likely to be mass-market publications that survive rather than the numerically smaller volumes of specialised esoteric books. Would we want Pagans in a thousand years to regard an ancient survival of a Dennis Wheatley or Teen Witch novel to be their sole Pagan equivalent of the Dead Sea Scrolls? Our love of the internet is a dangerous process: websites and e-mails rarely survive their author's demise. So, what can we do?

Leaving time capsules could be an option, although I would love to be a fly on the wall of a Pagan committee deciding what went in! We can bequeath our ritual artefacts to a specialist museum, such as the Museum of Witchcraft and Magic in Cornwall or the Doreen Valiente Foundation. More research on our founding fathers and mothers needs to be done. Professor Ronald Hutton (1993, 1996, 1999, 2003, 2013 & 2017) and Phillip Heselton (2000, 2003, 2016 & others) have done some sterling research and publishing, but it should not all be left to them. Still, already some of the memories about our Pagan pioneers are fading and dying with their contemporaries. Others need to record their memories and experiences before they are lost.

Future Developments
Paganism can be like travel on a personal level: the journey is more important than the destination, and no doubt some will enjoy it and some not. As research continues, no doubt some more metaphorical 'sacred cows' will need to be slaughtered and practices adapted to an ever-changing world. Certainly, we seem to be at a developmental stage where more Pagans need to think about, discuss, and write about theology and ethics.

Within my lifetime Information Technology has completely changed (for better or worse) the way we do things. I suspect the technical world we marvel at today will be considered primitive in 50 years. Over the last twelve months, the international Coronavirus crisis has resulted in nearly all Pagan conferences, moots and camps being cancelled or postponed. However, some enterprising event organisers have set up successful virtual events, with online lectures, workshops, rituals, debates, and entertainment. Once we all get back to meeting each other again, I do not doubt that most events will switch back to a live format because the social interaction with other Pagans is as essential as content at such events.

Still, the online experience has shown a couple of advantages. As a speaker, I have been invited to contribute to events in India and the USA, which otherwise would generally be prohibitively expensive. Pagans who cannot travel due to health, distance, family, work and animal commitments and cost could also participate from their homes. Whether this will lead to more online events or live events simultaneously streaming to the internet remains to be seen. It could be a trend to watch out for in the future,

Political systems and countries have radically altered in some locations in the last few decades, and this may well continue, especially where prosperity and resources are so unevenly distributed. As a result, some authorities may be less or more tolerant of Paganism, particularly if they perceive it has a political agenda such as environmental issues or women's rights.

Global warming, pollution, ecological and natural disasters, starvation, disease, wars and water shortage are just some of the factors likely to change the earth, even more so if we continue to do nothing practical about it. As individuals, the task can be daunting, but we can alter what happens in our small corner. We should also take heart at the voices of conscience like David Attenborough, Greta Thunberg and Malala Yousafzai and how much of their messages are regarded by the world. They are of no value, though, if they are not turned into practical actions quickly.

Christianity has declined sharply in the last two decades in the UK and USA. Several countries are becoming more secular, with many people declaring themselves as not part of any religion. The situation in other countries seems less volatile. If Paganism continues to expand in the same manner, the number of Pagans worldwide will become significant. I do not believe it will ever be a mass religion again as there must be a saturation point for when all the likely open-minded, nature-loving, independent-thinking people are reached. Cynically I would state that it will only ever be a small percentage of any population, and visibly even less where the state controls or works hand in hand with religion!

One of the significant changes I would like to see in my lifetime is separating governments from religions since I believe there will not be any true religious equality until then. Some countries such as the USA have it officially, but there is heavy bias in reality which is only gradually being broken down. Kraemer predicts that Pagans may eventually follow the example of other persecuted minorities such as Mormons and LGBT+ and move towards living in the same area of America:

> *"Perhaps Pagans are less willing to compromise, or just not afraid for their lives, but it is a rare Pagan who will change jobs or move in order to be physically closer to other Pagans. Despite there being an estimated 1.2 million of us in the United States, Pagans often remain scattered and isolated, and we turn to the internet to find like-minded others. Online community is certainly better than nothing, but it will not help us raise our children or bring us potluck dishes when we bury our dead; the bonding that occurs when neighbors can casually run into each other at the grocery store cannot happen. As a movement, we do not prioritize Pagan*

> *community highly enough to make the sacrifice of moving—at least, not yet."*
>
> (Kraemer, C. 2014)

Oddly enough, living near several USAAF bases in England, I know that many American Pagan military service members try to get transfers to particular postings where they know there are already thriving Pagan communities. Some even have 'temple' buildings provided by the US when numbers are sufficient. I have talked to some and understand there are postings in some other countries with a similar Pagan reputation.

Paganism is already seen as 'the enemy' by some Christian spokespersons, such as the Catholic priest who warns against *"Introducing the new threat: global neo-paganism."* (Father Dwight Longenecker, 2019) The National Secular Society reported on Scottish Evangelists from the Solas Centre for Public Christianity with a headline: *'Scottish evangelists identify Paganism as one of the "biggest threats to Western civilisation!"* '(McBay, A., 2015). These attacks could be giving us delusions of grandeur, prompting others to check that we are not terrorists or some sinister global conspiracy, but we have more sense than that. (We may have to stop joking about pentagrams being 'Wiccan Death Stars!') Seriously though, as our movement becomes more significant, it becomes more of a threat to those whose religion is receding. Sadly, I do not think that these will be the last attacks.

When Cara Schulz (2016), a journalist with The Wild Hunt, asked American Pagans to say how they thought Pagan culture would develop amongst the variety of answers. Phaedra Bonewits thought that *"Occult practitioners in general may be pushed far to the outside of Paganism as worship-focused Paganism becomes more the norm ... Generic, nature-focused Pagans may be seen as a quaint artefact from the 20th century. Those who attempt 20th-century coven-*

The Pagan Thinker

based, initiatory mystery religion Wicca will be a tiny minority, just as members of magical lodges are today. The Wheel of the Year may become quaint, too, lost in favour of holy days specific to deities being honoured."

Selena Fox thought that *"There will be more Pagan sacred places established, owned and cared for by Pagan organizations — more stone circles, shrines, temples, retreat centres, libraries, cemeteries, groves, and Nature sanctuaries. …There will be more Pagans serving in elected public office in local, state, and federal forms of government. Having one's Pagan orientation known will seldom be a concern raised as an issue during elections as it has been in the 20th & 21st centuries."*

Druid John Beckett warned, *"Something we think is certain will fail, and something we aren't even considering will arise. If we are wise, we will focus on being the best Witches, Pagans, polytheists, and such as we possibly can. Strong practices and resilient communities can succeed in any environment."*

Jason Mankey, a Gardnerian Witch, thought, *"Today we sometimes talk about the Pagan umbrella having some 'leaks,' in one hundred years I think the umbrella will be long gone, with many groups and traditions distancing themselves from the word 'Pagan.'"*

There were many more interesting comments and predictions within that Wild Hunt article: you could probably add your own. Unfortunately, I concur with many that a larger Pagan population will undoubtedly lead to more fragmentation.

> *Within particular Pagan communities, any marked growth in membership is likely to place serious strains on organizational structures. Modern Pagans have proven resistant to centralized leadership and organization, with a preference for small, local, or regional units and a tendency to split into still smaller factions when disputes and personality conflicts arise*

The Pagan Thinker

(Strmiska, M., 2005 p.47)

Hitherto hidden traditions such as the Italian Janare[42] could re-emerge and become popularised. In addition, some of the presently less popular little-known UK folk traditions, such as Cunning Man, Horse Whisperer or Toadman, may be revived.

The numerical quantity of new Pagans could also reduce the overall quality of people coming forward. Some people will simply say *'me too'* without thinking about it too deeply, possibly producing an elitist reaction from some more established Pagans.

Therefore, Intrafaith initiatives between the various Pagan groupings will become more important to reach consensus and mediate disputes. There will be a continuing need for Interfaith dialogue between religions, especially in those parts of the world where it has not become established yet.

> *"Modern Paganism is very young. To remain far into the future, we must be a living religion -- one that thrives and changes its social structure, ritual style, and content; one that meets the different needs of each new generation."*

(Masery, 2010)

Politically it could be helpful to have a louder voice to achieve Pagan aims of religious equality, environmentally-friendly policies such as recycling and limited development of green sites, better recognition of feminist agendas, preservation of ancient sacred sites and creation of new ones. So a larger body of people is less likely to be ignored, particularly when voting is marginal. Yet that may make us increasingly politicised, which is a mixed blessing. If we are seen as influencers, both political and commercial players are likely to subvert the process.

If some of the issues that Pagans have been banging on about for years, such as recycling, become commonplace, maybe they will become a less visible sign of a Pagan lifestyle and more the standard expectation for whole communities. It may be interesting to speculate whether they would have ever got to that situation without the protests, campaigning and goading of Pagans and other environmental activists?

However, just as any popular protest march is likely to be infiltrated by other factions anxious to piggyback their causes and be seen as more representative, Paganism's infiltration and subversion will become more prevalent. Heathenry has had the problem of far-right neo nazi's trying to use it as a recruiting ground for years across Europe and the USA.[43] I understand that Communist groups have targeted Druidry in France and elsewhere. National security services become aware of such actions and are likely to react accordingly; it is the job they are paid to do. In some cases, they are even tipped off by Pagans worried about what is happening and may infiltrate suspect groups themselves.

Helen A. Berger reported that in two surveys (based on about 8000 informants) she conducted in the USA, there was an increasing number of solitary practitioners. They had mainly learned about Paganism from books and the internet and did not belong to any group. However, most of them communicated with other Pagans, and many attended festival events. (Berger, H. 2010) There does not appear to be any comparable survey elsewhere in Western Paganism.

This last chapter is mainly my supposition, and I think that others can produce far cleverer answers to what will happen in Paganism's future. It doesn't matter much to me, as I am already in my senior years and so am unlikely to see much of it, although I fervently hope that will be a good one. However, that is not the point. The far more critical question, is what do you think YOU will be doing in the future? If you want to know what the future holds, make it yourself. For example, at the Pagan Federation 40th Anniversary, in 2011, the Druid Philip Carr-Gomm said:

"In the end, Paganism will become what each of us makes of it. The magician stands as a Hermes figure mediating between this world and the Otherworld."

(Carr-Gomm, P. 2011)

The Pagan Thinker

Bibliography & References

Aburrow, Y., (2008) *Do Pagans see their beliefs as compatible with science?*
https://www.academia.edu/4556936/Do_Pagans_see_their_beliefs_as_compatible_with_science Accessed 29/03/21

Aburrow, Y. (2010) *What would a contemporary Pagan theology look like?*
http://pagantheologies.pbworks.com/w/page/13622178/Pagan%20theology Accessed 31/03/21

Adams, N. (2021) *Sacred Sites*
https://www.reonline.org.uk/resources/sacred-sites/ Accessed 19/03/21

Adler, M. (2009) Margot Adler IN Vale & Sulak (Eds) *Modern Pagans* San Francisco, USA: Research Publications

Adler, R. (1979) *Drawing Down the Moon* USA: Viking Press

Anczyk, A. & Vencálek, M. (2013) *Coming Home to Paganism: Theory of Religious Conversion or a Theological Principle? Studia Religiologica* 46 (3) 2013, s. 161–171

Aradia, S. (2013)*Your Mileage May Vary – Embracing Contradictory Truths in the Craft.*
http://www.patheos.com/blogs/agora/2013/11/seekers-and-guides-your-mileage-may-vary-embracing-contradictory-truths-in-the-craft November 25, 2013. (Accessed 16/03/21)

Ashear, V. (2018) *Five Big Theological Questions for Everyone* http://uucasper.org/services/five-big-theological-questions-everyone/ Accessed 28/03/21

Aspren, E. (2008) Heathens Up North: Politics, Polemics, and Contemporary Norse Paganism in Norway *The Pomegranate* 10.1 (2008) 41-69

Barrett, F. (1801) *The Magus* https://www.sacred-texts.com/grim/magus/

Prof. Bates, B. (1983) *The Way of the Wyrd* London: Hay House

Bahnisch, A. (2001) *Sociology of Religion in Postmodernity: Wicca, Witches and the neo-pagan Myth of Foundations*

TASA 2001 Conference, The University of Sydney, 13-15 December 2001

Beckett, J. (2016) *A Pagan Crisis of Faith* https://www.patheos.com/blogs/johnbeckett/2016/10/a-pagan-crisis-of-faith.html Accessed 30/03/21

Becket, Maynard & Jordan (2017) *Values and Ethics in Social Work. 3rd edition.* London: Sage

Berger, H. (2010) *Are Solitaries The Future Of Paganism?* https://www.patheos.com/resources/additional-resources/2010/08/solitaries-the-future-of-paganism Accessed 22/03/21

Birchall, B. (2010) *Re-enchanting the landscape: Neo-Pagan engagement with prehistoric sites.* (dissertation, UK.)

'Black Witch' (2014) I'm a black Pagan, would you date me? https://afropunk.com/2010/12/im-a-black-pagan-would-you-date-me/ Accessed 30/03/21

Blain, J. and Wallis, R (2004) Sites, Texts, Contexts and Inscriptions of Meaning: Investigating Pagan 'Authenticities' in a Text-Based Society *The Pomegranate 6.2 (2004) 231-252*

Blain, J. and Wallis, R (2008). Sacred, secular, or sacrilegious? Prehistoric sites, pagans and the Sacred Sites project in Britain. In: Schachter & Brockman, (eds.) *(Im)permanence: Cultures In/Out of Time.* Pittsburg, Penn State University Press, 212-223.

Bly, R. (1990) *Iron John.* New York: Addison-Wesley

Bogdan, H. (2006) Challenging the Morals of Western Society. IN *The Pomegranate* 8.2 (2006) 211-246

Bonewits, I. (1989) *Real Magic* Maine, USA: Samuel Weiser

Bonewits, I. (2005) *The Pagan Man*: Priests, *Warriors, Hunters and Drummers.* New York, USA: Citadel

Bord, J&C (1976) *The Secret Country* London: Book Club Associates

Briggs, R. (1996). *Witches & Neighbours: the social and cultural context of European Witchcraft.* London: Harper Collins

Brown, A. (2021) *Moral Principles And How They Impact Your Life* https://www.betterhelp.com/advice/behavior/moral-principles-and-how-they-impact-your-life/ *07/10/20*

Bryant, A. (2016) Educating Hampshire – One Woman's Attempt to 'Normalise' Paganism IN Brown, N. (Ed) *Pagan Planet* Alresford: Moon Books

Butler, E. (2012) *Essays on a Polytheistic Philosophy of Religion.* New York: Phaidra Editions

Carr-Gomm, P. (2011) *The future of Paganism* www.philipcarr-gomm.com/essay/future-paganism/ Accessed 04/04/21

Campion, N. (2004) *Prophesy, Cosmology and the New Age movement: the extent and nature of contemporary belief in astrology.* Bath: Bath Spa University College https://core.ac.uk/download/pdf/29422385.pdf 18/08/2020

Chandler, I. (2016) PaganAid and the road to social justice. IN Brown, N. (Ed) *Pagan Planet* Alresford: Moon Books

Cochrane, R. & Jones, E.J. (2002) *The Robert Cochrane Letters: An insight into Modern Traditional Witchcraft* (Ed. Howard, M.) Chievely: Capall Bann

Cooper, A. (1997) *Sacred Mountains: ancient wisdom and modern meanings.* Edinburgh: Floris Books

Corringham, I. (2019) *Magic and religion* ADF https://www.adf.org/articles/cosmology/discussing-pagan-theology.html Accessed 17/03/21

Cornish, H. (2009) Spelling Out History: Transforming Witchcraft Past and Present in *The Pomegranate* 11.1 (2009) 14-28

Crowley, V. (2002) Carl Jung and the Development of Contemporary Paganism in *The Development of Paganism: History, Influences and Contexts, 1880-2002* UK: Open University.

Cusack, C. (2020) *Prehistoric Monuments as Numinous Sites of Spiritual Tourism: The Rollright Stones.* Australia: University of Sydney

Cush, D (2019) *Contemporary Paganism in the UK*
https://www.bl.uk/sacred-texts/articles/contemporary-paganism-in-the-uk# Accessed 16/03/21

diZerega, G. *NeoPaganism, Divine Immanence, and the Sacred Feminine*
https://www.dizerega.com/2020/08/10/neopaganism-divine-immanence-and-the-sacred-feminine/?fbclid=IwAR1w-cDXn1WBnyUvCGkrr9oHHW6d784v9ozGtJt9dOgbArluSt-NYrR0VCw Accessed 05/03/21

diZerega G. *Will the Real Pagan Theology Please Stand Up*?
https://www.beliefnet.com/columnists/apagansblog/2009/03/will-the-real-pagan-theology-please-stand-up.html Accessed 15/03/21

Foster, C. (2010) *Wired For God?: The biology of spiritual experience* London: Hodder & Stoughton

Franklin, A.,(2017) *Maiden, Mother, Crone?*
https://annafranklinhearthwitch.wordpress.com/2017/02/21/maiden-mother-crone/ Accessed 05/04/21

Frazer, Sir James G. (1890) *The Golden Bough*, London: Macmillan

Gault, M. (2015) *How is Community Constructed in Neo-Paganism?*
https://www.academia.edu/18541500/How_is_Community_Constructed_in_Neo_Paganism Accessed 27/03/21

Gecewicz, C., (2018) *New Age' beliefs common among both religious and nonreligious Americans*
https://www.pewresearch.org/fact-tank/2018/10/01/new-age-beliefs-common-among-both-religious-and-nonreligious-americans/ Accessed 20/03/21

Gracyck, T. *Four fundamental ethical principles*
http://web.mnstate.edu/gracyk/courses/phil%20115/Four_Basic_principles.htm Accessed 05/03/21

Green, M. (2018) *The Pitfall of Consumer Paganism*
https://atheopaganism.wordpress.com/2018/06/15/the-pitfall-of-consumer-paganism/ Accessed 30/03/21

Grieve, G., (1995) Imagining a Virtual Religious Community: Neo-Pagans and the Internet *Chicago Anthropology Exchange* Vol. 21 (7) 98-132

Gruben, M (2017) *Circle-casting basics: All you need to know about magick circles* https://www.groveandgrotto.com/blogs/articles/circle-casting-basics-all-you-need-to-know-about-magick-circles Accessed 25/03/21

Guest, C. (1997) *The Mabinogion* New York: Dover

Gulik, L. (2017) *Moongazers and Trailblazers: Creative dynamics in Low Country Wicca. Netherlands*: Leiden University

Hale, B. (2012) *Sacred Spaces and Sensual Selves: the use of liminal space and sexual symbols in the creation of erotic identities at contemporary pagan festivals.* USA: MA Thesis for The University of Chicago

Halstead, J. (2015) *The Greening of Paganism: The Place of 'A Pagan Community Statement on the Environment' in the history of contemporary Paganism* https://www.academia.edu/Documents/in/Pagan_Theology Accessed 16/03/21

Harner, M. (1982) *The Way of the Shaman* New York, USA: Bantam

Harrington, M, (2015) Reflecting on Studying Wicca from within the Academy and the Craft: An Autobiographical Perspective in *The Pomegranate* 17.1 (2015)

Harvey, G. (2005) *Animism: Respecting the Living World* USA: Univ. of Columbia

Harvey, G. 1999) Coming Home and Coming Out Pagan but not Converting IN *Lamb C. and Bryant, D. (eds.), Religious Conversion: Contemporary Practices and Controversies (Issues in Contemporary Religion.)* London: Continuum

Harvey, G. & Hardman, (1995) *Paganism Today* London: Thorsons

Haseman, M. (2018) *How to Set a Magickal Intention* https://www.mumblesandthings.com/blog/magical-intention Accessed 26/03/21

Hawkins, J. (2018) *Elemental Spirits* London: Golbin

Hedenborg-White, M. (2014) Contemporary Paganism. IN. Lewis, R. and Petersen, J. (eds.), *Controversial New Religions, 2nd ed*. Oxford: Oxford University Press,

Heselton, P (2000) *Wiccan Roots: Gerald Gardner and the modern Witchcraft revival*. Milverton: Capall Bann

Heselton, P (2003) *Gerald Gardner and the Cauldron of Inspiration* Milverton: Capall Bann

Heselton, P. (2016) *Doreen Valiente: Witch* London: Doreen Valiente Foundation

Hume, L. (1998) Creating Sacred Space: Outer Expressions of Inner Worlds in Modern Wicca *Journal of Contemporary Religion*, Vol.13, No.3 p. 309-319

Hutton, R. (1993) *The Pagan Religions of the Ancient British Isles: Their Nature and Legacy*. Oxford: Blackwell.

Hutton, R. (1996) *The Stations of the Sun: a history of the ritual year in Britain.* Oxford: Oxford University Press

Hutton, R. (1999) *The Triumph of the Moon: A History of Modern Pagan Witchcraft*. Oxford: Blackwell.

Hutton, R. (2003) *Witches, Druids and King Arthur*. London: Hambledon & London.

Hutton, R. (2008) Modern Pagan Festivals: A Study in the Nature of Tradition IN *Folklore*, 119:3, 251-273

Hutton, R. (2013) *Pagan Britain* USA: Yale University Press

Hutton, R. (2017) *The Witch* USA: Yale University Press

IrreverentPriest, (2018) r/pagan online chat group https://www.reddit.com/r/pagan/comments/68uari/pagan_theol ogians/ Accessed 17/03/21

Jackson, N. & Howard, M. (2000) *The Pillars of Tubal-Cain Chievely:* Capall Bann

Jamison, I. (2011) *Embodied Ethics and Contemporary Paganism UK:* Open University

Jennings, P. (2002) *Pagan Paths: A Guide to Wicca, Druidry, Asatru, Shamanism and Other Pagan Practices*. London: Rider

Jennings, P. (2019). *Pathworking and Creative Visualisation*. Halstead: Gruff

Jennings, P. (2019) *Heathen Paths* (2nd revised expanded edition) Halstead: Gruff

Johnson, T. (1996) *Hidden Heritage: Discovering Ancient Essex* Chievely: Capall Bann

Jones, E.J. *(Ed. Howard, M.)* (2001) *The Roebuck in the Thicket*. Chievely: Capall Bann

Jones, E.J. *(Ed. Howard, M.)* (2003) *The Robert Cochrane Letters*. Chievely: Capall Bann

Jory, T.S. (2016) *Men's Place in Contemporary Paganism: Christian and Mythopoetic Influences*

Jung, C. (1968) *Man and His Symbols* USA: Dell

Kaldera, Raven. (2012) *Dealing with Deities: Practical Polytheistic Theology.* USA Hubbardston, MA: Asphodel Press

Kelly, A. (1991) *Crafting the Art of Magic, Book I: A History of Modern Witchcraft, 1939-1964* USA: Llewellyn Publications

Kinsella, K (2002) *The Tain: Translated from the Irish Epic Tain Bo Cuailnge* Oxford: Oxford University Press

Knight, S., & Ellwood, T., (2016) *The Pagan Leadership Anthology: An Exploration of Leadership and Community in Paganism and Polytheism* USA: Megalithica Books

Konieczny, P. (2018) Volunteer Retention, Burnout and Dropout in Online Voluntary Organizations: Stress, Conflict and Retirement of Wikipedians *in Research in Social Movements, Conflicts and Change*, Vol. 42, Emerald Publishing Limited, pp. 199-219. https://www.emerald.com/insight/content/doi/10.1108/S0163-786X20180000042008/full/html Accessed 09/03/21

Kraemer, C. (2012) *Seeking the Mystery: An Introduction to Pagan Theologies*. USA, Englewood, CO: Patheos

Kraemer, C. (2014) *The Future of Paganism (Part Two): What Pagans Can Learn from Pioneer Mormons* https://dowsingfordivinity.com/2014/03/31/the-future-of-paganism-part-two-what-pagans-can-learn-from-pioneer-mormons/ Accessed 04/04/21

Prof. La Fontaine (1998) *The Extent and Nature of Organised and Ritual Abuse: Research Findings, and Speak of the Devil:*

Tales of Satanic Abuse in contemporary England. Cambridge: Cambridge University Press

Laubach, M. (2007) The Epistemology of Esoteric Culture: Spiritual Claim-Making within the American Neopagan Community. *Journal of Alternative Spiritualities and New Age Studies,* Vol 3 p.45

Law, D. (2017) *How Do Pagans Construct Their Religious Identity? A Thematic Analysis* https://www.academia.edu/39805430/How_Do_Pagans_Const ruct_Their_Religious_Identity_A_Thematic_Analysis?auto=do wnload&email_work_card=download-paper Accessed 29/03/21

Letcher, A.(2004) Raising the Dragon: Folklore and the Development of Contemporary British Eco-Paganism in *The Pomegranate* 6.2 (2004) 175-198

Letcher, A (2015) *Paganism and the British Folk Revival citing* Hume and McPhillips, eds,(2006) *Popular Spiritualities: Politics of Contemporary Enchantment* Aldershot: Ashgate Publishing

Lewis, J. & Peterson, J. (2014) *Controversial New Religions* Oxford: Oxford Scholarship Online

Liddell, W.E. & Howard, M. (1994) *The Pickingill Papers: the origin of the Gardnerian Craft.* Chievely: Capall Bann

Longenecker, D. (2019) *Introducing the new threat: Global neo-paganism.* https://dwightlongenecker.com/introducing-the-new-threat-global-neo-paganism/ Accessed 22/03/21

Magliocco, S., (2004). *Witching Culture: Folklore and Neo-paganism in America.* Philadelphia, USA: University of Pennsylvania Press

Magliocco, S. (2021) *Italian American Stregheria and Wicca: Ethnic Ambivalence in American Neopaganism* USA: University of Pennsylvania Press

Masery, (2010) *The Future of Paganism Is Our Future* *https://www.patheos.com/resources/additional-resources/2010/08/future-of-paganism-is-our-future?p=3* Accessed 22/03/21

Massei, K. (2017) *School of the Elemental Beings* London: Rudolf Steiner Press

McBay, A. (2015) *Scottish evangelists identify Paganism as one of the "biggest threats to Western civilisation."* https://www.secularism.org.uk/opinion/2015/11/scottish-evangelists-identify-paganism-as-one-of-the-biggest-threats-to-western-civilisation Accessed 27/03/2021

Mcintyre, J. (2016) *My Experience as a Pagan in Modern Scotland* http://www.understandingtheology.org/2016/10/my-experience-as-a-pagan-in-modern-scotland/ Accessed 17/03/21

McKay-Riddell, V. (2021) *Five Essential Traits of Pagan Leaders https://www.cherryhillseminary.org/five-essential-traits-of-pagan-leaders/* Accessed 19/03/21

Meuler, M. (2005) *Kore in Conflict: Feminist Neo-Pagans Look the Other Way As the God Rapes the Goddess*

Monnastre, C. & Griffin, D (1995) *Israel Regardie, initiation and psychotherapy.* https://auroradorada.com/en/regardie.htm accessed 04/03/21

Morehead, J.(2006) *Daughters of the Moon: Eclectic Mormon Women and Their Search for a Place in the Light of the Sun* https://www.academia.edu/2049646/Eclectic_Mormon_Women_Ethnography_paper?email_work_card=view-paper Accessed 04/04/21

Morgan, C.(2021) *The Nature of Sin* https://www.thegospelcoalition.org/essay/the-nature-of-sin/ Accessed 23/03/21

Morris, B. (2006) *Religion and Anthropology: a critical introduction.* Cambridge: Cambridge University Press

Murray, M.A. (1933), *The God of the Witches*. Oxford: Oxford University Press.

Nichols, R. (1991) *The Book of Druidry* London: Aquarian

Oringderff & Schaefer (2007) *Spiritual Philosophy and Practice of Wicca in the U.S. Military* Texas, USA: The Sacred Well Congregation

Pagan & Heathen Symposium (2015) *Pagan And Heathen Events Code of Conduct* https://pagansymposium.org Accessed 13/03/2021

Panin, S. (2015) Discussions on Pagan Theology *in the Academia and in the Pagan Community in Mediterranean Journal of Social Sciences, MCSER Rome-Italy* Vol 6 No 3 p.602-606

Patheos.com, (2021) *Religion Library, Paganism: Leadership 2021* https://www.patheos.com/library/pagan/ethics-morality-community/leadershipclergy

Patterson, R. (2018) *The Maiden, Mother, Crone debate* https://www.patheos.com/blogs/beneaththemoon/2018/08/the-maiden-mother-crone-debate/ Accessed 05/04/21

Pearson, N. (2015) *The Devil's Plantation: East Anglian lore, witchcraft and folk magic.* London: Troy Books

Pennick, N. (2004) *Secrets of East Anglian Magic Chievely*: Capall Bann

Pitzl-Waters, J. (2013) *Pagans and Interfaith Dialog* https://wildhunt.org/2013/03/pagans-and-interfaith-dialog.html Accessed 30/03/21

Poole, R. (ed), (2003) *The Lancashire Witches: Histories and Stories.* Manchester: Manchester University Press

Rankin, D. & Este, S. & (2008) *Practical Elemental Magick: Working the Magick of Air Fire Water & Earth in the Western Esoteric Tradition* London: Avalonia

Rathouse, W. (2021) *Contested Heritage: Relations between contemporary Pagan groups and the archaeological and heritage professions in Britain in the early 21st century* Oxford: BAR publishing

Reece, G., (2017) *Pagan Leaders and Clergy: A Quantitative Exploration* IN The *Pomegranate, the International Journal of Pagan Studies* VOL 19, NO 1 (2017)

Restall Orr, E. (2008) *Living with Honour: A Pagan Ethics* London: O Books

Rutherford, L., (2011) *Who is / what is a shaman?* https://eagleswing.co.uk/articles/contemporary-shamanism/ Accessed 05/04/21

Scherer, Allen & Harp. (2016) Grin and bear it: An examination of volunteers' fit with their organization, burnout and spirituality *Burnout Research, Volume 3, Issue 1, March 2016, Pages 1-10*

Schulz, C. (2016) *What will Paganism look like in 100 years?* https://wildhunt.org/2016/01/what-will-paganism-look-like-in-100-years.html Accessed 22/03/21

Scott, M. *Fierce tenderness and White Horse Hill woman: the teachings of Carolyn Hillyer.* https://accidentalgods.life/fierce-IN
tenderness/?fbclid=IwAR0KAeGFfQg8rr3c1ulINq3EKEQPB5lx
mYE8uTCvOT6qGXfTI-VRfoQ2l1I Accessed 05/03/21

Starhawk (2001) Starhawk IN (Ed. Vale & Sulak) *Modern Pagans* San Francisco, USA: Research Publications

Starhawk (1979) *The Spiral Dance: a Rebirth of the Ancient Religion of the Great Goddess* USA: Harper

Stewart, R.J. (2009) *Merlin: the Prophetic Vision and Mystic Life*, London: RJ Stewart Books

Strmiska, M., (2005) *Modern Paganism in World Cultures: Comparative Perspectives* USA: ABC-CLIO

Stubba (1991) *The Book of Blots: Ceremonies, Rituals & Invocations of the Odinic Rite.* London: The Odinic Rite

Sturluson, S. (1991) *Heimskringla: History of the Kings of Norway* USA: University of Texas

Sturluson, S. (2015) *The Prose Edda* London: Benediction Classics

Stygal, M. (2014) *Paganism and Interfaith in the UK and Europe* The Interfaith Observer, December 15, 2019.

Swami Vivekananda, (1998) *Karma-Yoga* India: Advaita Ashrama, Calcutta.

Thomas, V. (2020) *Of Chalk and Flint: a way of Norfolk magic* London: Troy Books

Sylvan, D.,(2007) *On crises of faith* https://diannesylvan.typepad.com/dancing_down_the_moon/2007/01/on_crises_of_fa.html Accessed 30/03/21

Titus, T., (2016) *Know Thyself, Serve Others – Effective Pagan Leadership* https://wildhunt.org/2016/07/column-know-thyself-serve-others-effective-pagan-leadership.html Accessed 18/03/21

Treadwell, C. (2013) *Facing the Darkness* Winchester: Moon Books

Trubshaw, B., (2021) *Paganism in British Folk Customs* https://www.indigogroup.co.uk/edge/paganism.htm Accessed 18/03/21

Urban, H. (2006) *Magia Sexualis: Sex, Magic, and Liberation in Modern Western Esotericism* USA: University of California

Valiente, D. (1961) *Where witchcraft lives London*: Aquarian

Wise, C. (2015) *Finding Elen: The Quest for Elen of the Ways* UK: Createspace

Wright, R., (2007) *Why is there evil and suffering?* https://www.christianitytoday.com/biblestudies/articles/evangelism/seven-questions-skeptics-ask.html Accessed 28/03/21

York, M. (2003) *Pagan Theology: Paganism as a world religion.*New York: New York University Press

Books & eBooks by Pete Jennings

Pathworking (with Pete Sawyer) – Capall Bann (1993)
Northern Tradition Information Pack – Pagan Federation (1996)
Supernatural Ipswich – Gruff (1997)
Pagan Paths – Rider (2002)
The Northern Tradition – Capall Bann (2003)
Mysterious Ipswich – Gruff (2003)
Old Glory & the Cutty Wren – Gruff (2003)
Pagan Humour – Gruff (2005)
The Gothi & the Rune Stave – Gruff (2005)
Haunted Suffolk – Tempus (2006)
Tales & Tours – Gruff (2006)
Haunted Ipswich – Tempus/ History Press (2010)
Penda: Heathen King of Mercia and his Anglo-Saxon World. – Gruff (2013)
The Wild Hunt & its followers – Gruff (2013)
Blacksmith Gods, Myths, Magicians & Folklore – Moon Books- Pagan Portals (2014)
Heathen Information Pack (with others) – Pagan Federation (2014)
Confidently Confused – Gruff (2014)
Adventures in Ælphame – Gruff (2015)
Valkyries, selectors of heroes: their roles within Viking & Anglo-Saxon heathen beliefs. - Gruff (2016)
A Cacophony of Corvids: the mythology, facts, behaviour and folklore of ravens, crows, magpies and their relatives. - Gruff (2017)
Heathen Paths: Viking and Anglo-Saxon Pagan Beliefs (2nd edition) – Gruff (2018)
The Bounds of Ælphame – Gruff (2019)
The Woodwose in Suffolk & beyond. – Gruff (2019)
Pathworking & Creative Visualisation – Gruff (2019)
Viking Warrior Cults – Gruff (2019)
When the sea turned to beer – Gruff (2019)
The Wyrd of Aelphame – Gruff (2020)

The Dog Walk Detectives – Gruff (2021)
Conveyor Belt Corpse – Gruff (2021)

Pete Jennings has also contributed with others to:
Modern Pagans: an investigation of contemporary Pagan practices. (Eds. V Vale & J. Sulak.) San Francisco: RE/Search (2001)
The Museum of Witchcraft: A Magical History – (Ed. Kerriann Godwin) Boscastle: Occult Art Co. (2011)
Heathen Information Pack – UK: Pagan Federation (2014)
The Call of the God: an anthology exploring the divine masculine within modern Paganism (Ed. Frances Billinghurst) Australia: TDM (2015)
Pagan Planet: Being, Believing & Belonging in the 21st Century. Ed. Nimue Brown. Moon Books (2016)

Recordings
Awake (with WYSIWYG) – Homebrew (1987) HB 8705
Chocks Away (with WYSIWYG) – Athos (1988) ATHOS 001
No Kidding (with Pyramid of Goats) – Gruff (1990) GRUFF001
Spooky Suffolk (with Ed Nicholls) Gruff (2003) GRUFFCD020
Old Glory & the Cutty Wren CD – Gruff (2003) GRUFFCD 021

Films that Pete has featured in
Suffolk Ghosts – Directed by Richard Felix. Past in Pictures, 2005
Wild Hunt – Directed by Will Wright. Film Tribe, 2006
In search of Beowulf with Michael Wood – BBC4, 2009
Born of Hope – Directed by Kate Maddison – Actors at Work 2010
The Last Journey – Directed by Carl Stickley 2018

Details of how to obtain these books and an up to date diary of lectures and appearances by Pete Jennings can be found at
www.gippeswic.org

Most books are available as hard copy and electronic digital versions via
www.amazon.co.uk/Pete-Jennings/e/B0034OPQP8

Pete regularly writes shorter magazine articles and reviews, especially for *Wiðowinde, Pagan Dawn*, *Witchcraft & Wicca*. He was also the editor of the *Gippeswic* magazine. You can also follow Pete Jennings & Ealdfaeder on Facebook. For appearances of Pete with his Ealdfaeder Anglo Saxons re-enactor friends, plus lots of information on Anglo Saxon topics, go to www.ealdfaeder.org

About Pete Jennings

Pete was born in Ipswich, Suffolk, England, in 1953. He retired as a registered Social Worker in 2019. He holds a BA (Hons) in Social Work (Anglia Ruskin University) and a Diploma in Professional Studies and Counselling (Anglia Polytechnic University.) He was an accredited Member of the British Association of Counsellors & Psychotherapists.

Pete was first the Media Officer and then President of The Pagan Federation, Europe's largest umbrella organisation for all forms of Paganism. He remains High Gothi of Odinshof and is an author, lecturer, folklorist, historian, actor, broadcaster and Anglo-Saxon re-enactor. He lives with his second wife, Sue. Between them, they have four adult offspring, nine grandchildren and a German Shepherd Dog called Sasha.

Some useful websites of organisations in the book.

Asatru UK (UK) https://www.asatruuk.org/
Atlantis Bookshop (UK) http://theatlantisbookshop.com/
British Druid Order (UK) https://www.druidry.co.uk/
Centre For Pagan Studies (UK) http://centre-for-pagan-studies.com/
Children of Artemis (CoA) (UK & Europe) https://witchcraft.org/
Covenant of the Goddess (Wiccan, USA) https://cog.org/
Circle Sanctuary (USA) https://www.circlesanctuary.org/
Druid Network (UK) https://druidnetwork.org/
Doreen Valiente Foundation (UK)
https://www.shop.doreenvaliente.org/
Eagles Wing Centre for Contemporary Shamanism (UK)
https://eagleswing.co.uk
Fellowship of Isis (International)
http://www.fellowshipofisis.com/
Heathen Pagan Symposium (UK)
https://pagansymposium.org/
Honouring the Ancient Dead (HAD)
https://www.honour.org.uk/
LifeRites (UK) http://www.liferites.org.uk/
Moonhenge (UK) http://www.moonhenge.co.uk/
Museum of Witchcraft & Magic (UK)
https://museumofwitchcraftandmagic.co.uk/
Olgar Trust (UK) https://www.olgartrust.org/
Order of Bards, Ovates & Druids (OBOD) (UK & Europe)
https://druidry.org/
PaganAid https://www.paganaid.org/
Pagan Federation (UK & Europe) https://www.paganfed.org/
Pomegranate (International)
https://journals.equinoxpub.com/index.php/POM
Sentry Circle (UK) https://www.sentrycircle.co.uk/
Treadwells Bookshop (UK) https://www.treadwells-london.com/
Watkins Bookshop (UK) https://watkinsbooks.com/
Wild Hunt (International) https://wildhunt.org/

[1] I am referring to Pagan Druids in this book. There are also Druids of other religions, including Christian and Buddhist.

[2] https://www.theguardian.com/world/2006/sep/04/religion.uk Accessed 07/03/21

[3] I gave a summary of many of the choices open to modern Western Pagans in my book 'Pagan Paths.' (Jennings, 2002)

[4] Uzzell, J. (2016) Work IN BROWN, N. (Ed) Pagan Planet Alresford: Moon Books p.127-129

[5] In Jungian theory, a primitive mental image inherited from the earliest human ancestors and supposed to be present in the collective unconscious.

[6] Present at the protest at Twyford Down outside Winchester, Hampshire. They became an influence on others.

[7] https://answers.yahoo.com/question/index?qid=20090622084539AAPb4lm&guccounter=1&guce_referrer=aHR0cHM6Ly93d3cuYmluZy5jb20v&guce_referrer_sig=AQAAACA9u06hyyVGtiNWmbKiD449Aj22_23vrCXggpnu_cpXSqjI5gcAojSgixESUWmCfyIJJhQJsh5m7GprcYjcQp3DhWBL626-h0JTPKsowwqQhA6P5X5TSZkGGMsu_LWAQqR2MU0h49ERHdgXafb5jwPgr1QzkTYQF6iUM4MvZ-Oe Accessed 26/03/21

[8] "Historically-informed Pagan religions are jigsaw puzzles which are missing pieces, which have enormous blank areas. What reconstructionist methodology enables us to do is to make informed, educated guesses to fill in those blank areas, based on the study of the data that we do have. This lets us direct ourselves properly in order to apply those themes in a contemporaneous sense to fill in the blanks for the present application of the religion" Lārhūs Fyrnsida (2021) On Religious Reconstruction within Paganism: A Methodological Defense https://larhusfyrnsida.com/ Accessed 26/03/21 [There are many contradictory statements about re-constructed Paganism, of which this is just one.]

[9] Developed in the 1970s by James Lovelock, it regards the Earth as a self regulating, living organism.

[10] Sharma, R. (2015) Not Five, but Nature has Six Elements https://www.modernagespirituality.com/not-five-but-nature-has-six-elements/ Accessed 24/03/21

[11] https://blog.oup.com/2019/02/how-six-elements-form-life-earth/ Accessed 24/03/21

[12] https://www.themystica.com/elementals/ Accessed 24/03/21

[13] Jaffa cakes are made by United Biscuits in the UK. They have a hard sponge bottom, orange flavour filling and chocolate flavoured topping. Occasionally they also produce a variety with lemon-lime flavour which are regarded as a heresy by some true believers!

[14] C.S. Lewis (1964) Reflections on the Psalms

[15] "The Neopagan movement is a dynamic religious movement under construction. It is a product of a convergence of non-Christian religions and the 1960s-1970s countercultural values, emphasising individualism, democratic empowerment, and entrepreneurialism – all of which resulted in a democratisation of revelation. However, these same values present problems in organising collective action around the resulting revelations because they impede the development of structures with which to collectively authorise the revelation. Neopagans resolve this by authorising revelations around which a consensus can develop and that solve collective problems. On an individual and organisational basis, Neopagans authenticate claims in a way that is similar to the early empiricists – by examining the claimant's social standing, the narrative structure of the claim, and the interests of the claimant and the judge."

[16] 'Burning Times' by Charlie Murphy on the vinyl LP *Catch the Fire* (1981) He later admitted that he had been genuinely mistaken in quoting 9 million. The song was later covered by Christy Moore and Roy Bailey.

[17] E.g. Prof Ronald Hutton, Dr. Mellissa Harington, Linda Sever, Dr. Jenny Blain, Michael York, Prof. Graham Hervey, Dr Christina Oakley-Harrington, Dr Joanne Pearson, Dr. Vivianne Crowley, Dr Melvyn Willin, Dr. Caroline Tully, Prof. Diane Purkiss and others I have omitted through ignorance or brevity..

[18]

http://rsnonline.org/index9438.html?option=com_content&view=article&id=892&Itemid=1009 Accessed 15/03/21

[19] 'Summerland's was a name given to the after life, pictured as an astral plane by the Theosiphists. It possibly originated with the Swedish author Emanuel Swedenborg (1688–1772)

[20] Contrary to popular belief, the warriors heaven Valhalla is only one of many halls of the dead in the mythological Norse afterlife. Each of the main gods seems to maintain one, such as Sessrumnir, the many seated family friendly heaven in the realm of Fólkvangr belonging to the Goddess Freyja.

[21] Lord Salisbury (1830-1903) in a letter to Lord Lyton 1877.

[22] https://www.patheos.com/library/pagan/ethics-morality-community/principles-of-moral-thought-and-action Accessed 27/03/21

[23] Usually accredited to *'In Memoriam'* (1850), by the English poet Alfred Tennyson (1809-92) but the actual phrase was in use before his poem. It is usually thought to mean Nature at its rawest, with competition leading to violence.

[24] Campion, N. (2004*) Prophesy, Cosmology and the New Age movement: the extent and nature of contemporary belief in astrology*. The Pew Forum on Religion and Public Life.

[25] Herbert Spencer (1891) *Essays, Volume 3 'Prison Ethics.'*

[26] Mosley, Shelley; Caggiano, Anna; Charles, John (October 15, 1996). "The "Self-Weeding" Collection: The Ongoing Problem of Library Theft, and How To Fight Back". *Library Journal*. 121 (171): 38–40.

[27] 'The Law of Threefold' return was said by his priestess Dorien Valiente to have been invented by Gerald Gardner, and I can find no trace of it prior to his writings. I have frequently challenged Pagans to produce historic precedent for it before 1950 without yielding a single contender.

[28] A few years ago when I was President of the Pagan Federation I met with the Secretary of the World Hindu Organisation from India and his UK representative. Almost the first words he said to me were "As two Pagan religions we have so much in common to talk about." Although Hinduism is frequently thought of as a single religion, it is a collection of hundreds of spiritual paths with a myriad of gods and goddeses.

[29] Kenneth Grant was a secretary to Aleister Crowley, who initiated him into the OTO. Grant later founded his own Thelemic organisation, the Typhonian Ordo Templi Orientis—later renamed the Typhonian Order—with his wife Steffi Grant.

[30] Antinomian: a person who believes that Christians are released by grace from the obligation of observing the moral law.

[31] Bird G. & Winkelstein, P. (October 2014) A comparative analysis of moral principles and behavioral norms in eight ethical codes relevant to health sciences librarianship, medical informatics, and the health professions *Journal of the Medical Library Association* 102(4). 247–256

[32] Moral Principles And How They Impact Your Life by Ashley Brown in https://www.betterhelp.com/advice/behavior/moral-principles-and-how-they-impact-your-life accessed 03/03/21

[33] Pluralism Project at Harvard University (2020) *Communal Worship, Rites of Passage* https://pluralism.org/communal-worship-rites-of-passage Accessed 05/04/21

[34] 1954, Washington. (Finest Hour 122, 15.). Misquoted by Harold MacMillan four years later as 'Jaw, jaw is better than war, war' during a trip to Australia. https://winstonchurchill.org/resources/quotes/quotes-falsely-attributed/ Accessed 20/03/21

[35] 'Inappropriate Sexuality: Sex Magic, S/M, and Wicca', in Theology & Sexuality 11(2), pp.31-42, 2005

[36] Simes, A. (1995*) Mercian Movements: Group transformation and individual choices amongst East Midlands Pagans.* In Harvey & Hardman (1995) pages 169-190*.*

[37] *'Profiles of the Future'*, 1962

[38] *'The Pillars of Tubal Cain'* is a good primer for Angelic magic by Jackson & Howard (2000)

[39] *"The Pickingill Papers"* by Liddell & Howard contains a series of controversial letters to the Cauldron magazine purporting to be involved in witchcraft before

Gardner. A further set of letters from Robert Cochrane (of the Clan of Tuball Cain) is contained in *"The Robert Cochrane Letters: An insight into modern Traditional Witchcraft"* by Cochrane & Evans (2002)

[40] Robert Cochrane's letter to William Gray.

[41] Valiente quoted in (Heselton 2000 p. 241) but there are other independent sources for this story I believe.

[42] Palmesano, M. (2021) Janare: Italian Witches of the Sacred Trees *Sacred Hoop Magazine issue 111 2021 p.40-43*

[43] See: Gardell, M. (2003) *Gods of the Blood: the Pagan revival and white separatism*. USA: Duke University Press

Printed in Great Britain
by Amazon

85375093R10105